Judy Brown's

GUIDE TO
NATURAL FOODS COOKING

by
Judy Brown
and
Dorothy R. Bates

D1552731

THE BOOK PUBLISHING COMPANY
SUMMERTOWN, TENNESSEE

Design: Eleanor Dale Evans

Photography: Thomas Johns

ISBN 0-913990-62-0   LCCC–89-552

© 1989 Judy Brown and Dorothy R. Bates

2 3 4 5 6 7 8 9 0

Brown, Judy A.
    Judy Brown's Guide to natural foods cooking

    Includes index.
    1. Cookery (Natural foods) I. Bates, Dorothy R.
II. Title. III. Title: Guide to natural foods cooking.
TX741.B76 1989   641.5'637   89-552
ISBN 0-913990-62-0

The Book Publishing Company
Summertown, TN 38483

Nutritional Analyses

Each recipe in this book has been analyzed for its calorie, protein, carbohy-drate and fat content, rounded up to the nearest gram or calorie. Optional ingredients, serving suggestions, garnishes and variations were not included. Also not included were unspecified quantities of basic ingredients, such as oil for preparing pans for baking, so these amounts could be determined by the individual. If a choice of two ingredients was listed, the first was selected for the analysis. If a range of servings or ingredient amounts was listed, such as 4-6 servings, an average of the two amounts was used.

CONTENTS

Introduction

For years people have been asking me "What got you into natural foods?" I would like to share my story of why I changed to a vegetarian, whole foods diet, and in turn, changed my entire lifestyle.

When I was 18, my Dad discovered he had cancer of the colon. Determined to save his life, I began to research everything I could on cancer; what created it, what made it continue to grow, what could be done to treat it. At the time I was into physical fitness and exercise but had not thought much about diet. To my amazement, I discovered a whole other world of nutrition, holistic health and preventive medicine.

According to a 1977 Senate Subcommittee on Nutrition, 7 out of 10 leading causes of death in this country could be related to diet. I learned of the problems of high fat diets (especially the saturated fats found mostly in meat and cheese) and studies indicating a correlation between too much fat in the diet and colon and breast cancer. I flashed on my Dad's heavy emphasis on meat. Like the old saying that holds true for many Americans, "He's a meat and potatoes man!"

I decided to eliminate meat from my own diet. Next went dairy products, sugar and refined, processed foods. For years I had suffered with severe headaches, insomnia and chronic lower back pain. Within a short time of changing my diet, my headaches and insomnia disappeared and eventually the backaches, too. I tried to persuade my Dad to change to a vegetarian diet. He made small changes, like eating brown rice and whole grain bread, miso soup and other foods. It was too difficult for him to make a total change-over at this point in his life. At age 55 he died after seven long years of battling cancer.

His illness and passing changed the focus of my life toward natural foods. My master's program in Consumer Economics at the University of Maryland focused on the economics of a healthy diet and lifestyle. My work as an economist at the US Department of Agriculture was spent studying the impact and growth of the natural foods industry in the US. I began to teach cooking classes to share with others what I had learned.

I can still hear my Dad saying to me, "You know, Judy, you should be photographing your natural foods dishes as you make them so you'll have the pictures all ready when you do a book one day." So here's to you, Dad! This book is dedicated to you. May it enhance the quality of life and good health of those who open its pages.

Judy A. Brown

Live Longer, Live Livelier

Medical research confirms what vegetarians have known for a long time, that there is a definite link between diet and good health. According to the Center for Science in the Public Interest, vegetarians lower their risks of developing a host of serious diseases. One small step at a time can lead to a big difference in eating habits. Look at it as an exciting challenge to prolong your life. Invest in your own "Living Life Insurance Policy" by following a healthy lifestyle.

Everything I read today says that people going from a meat-based diet to a plant-based diet should do so slowly. Some people's digestive systems take longer than others to adapt to manufacturing blood from plant protein vs. animal. As their bodies adapt to digesting so many complex carbohydrates, some initial weight loss is not unusual. If you exercise and eat well, your body finds the level of calorie intake it needs to match the calories expended.

Meal planning on a natural foods diet gives you freedom from the standard meat and potato format. Instead of a single food providing all the protein, carbohydrates or vitamins in a meal, whole foods give you a creative source for a mixture of nutrients. For example, grains can provide the protein for a meal in pilaf (pg. 98), or carbohydrates in a main dish vegetable pie (pg. 92) or rice pudding (pg. 146).

Principles to remember when changing over to a natural foods diet are:
• There is a truth to the saying "You are what you eat." Your health is affected by your diet, along with your relationships, home life, attitude, lifestyle, your enjoyment of your work and your level of physical activity.
• Look at cooking as "Cooking for your health." Your cooking can affect your biological destiny and those you cook for.
• Be happy when you prepare meals. You impart energy into the foods you are cooking and you want it to be positive.
• Eat locally grown foods as much as possible. They'll be fresher and you have a greater chance of knowing whether they were sprayed with pesticides.
• Eat organically grown foods as much as possible.
• Eat according to the seasons. During the winter months the body needs to take in foods that impart warmth, such as hot soups, stews, etc. In the hotter months the body can cool off by eating more fruits, raw salads, cold pasta, etc.
• Chew your food well to help your digestive system.
• Never go to bed on a full stomach; allow two hours for digestion.
• Don't overeat.
• Eat according to your constitution and your condition. Your constitution is what you inherited. Your condition has to do with your current state of health, your lifestyle, and whether you lead an active or sedentary life.

Your Nutritional Needs on a Natural Foods Diet

One of the main concerns people have when switching to a natural foods diet is getting enough protein. Actually some research shows most Americans are consuming too much protein, even some vegetarians. Consumers eating the Standard American diet are getting about twice as much protein as they need. Excessive protein consumption can lead to leaching of calcium and minerals from the bones, causing osteoporosis and the formation of kidney stones. Too much protein also contributes to deterioration of the kidneys, and can cause a build up of uric acid which can lead to gout. Tumor growth is also stimulated by consuming too much protein.

A vegetarian diet based on grains, legumes, soyfoods and vegetables provides your body with adequate protein. Protein is made up of amino acids. Eating beans and grains in the same meal compliments the amino acids they each contain and increases the total amount of protein available for your use. In the 1970's vegetarians thought it was very important to combine beans and grains at every meal to get enough protein in their diet. As nutritional research becomes more sophisticated, we've learned that these foods can adequately stand alone in much of your meal planning. Soy bean products (soymilk, tofu, tempeh and soy yogurt) are a complete protein, with all the essential amino acids, as well as iron, calcium and vitamin B. They are a good choice for growing children, pregnant mothers, athletes, someone recovering from illness or anyone who has higher than normal nutritional needs.

A Recommended Daily Allowance (RDA) of protein is now about 44 grams for a woman and 56 grams for a man, although many authorities think that substantially less is healthier. The protein content of some typical foods is:

1 cup cooked brown rice = 3.8 grams
1 cup cooked kidney beans = 14.4 grams
2 Tbsp. peanut butter = 7.8 grams
¼ lb. tofu = 8 grams
1 cup soy milk = 8.9 grams
2 oz. soy cheese = 6 grams
2 slices whole wheat bread = 4.4 grams
2 corn tortillas = 4.2 grams
½ cup cooked oatmeal = 3 grams
1 cup cooked pasta = 7.3 grams
½ cup cooked mung bean sprouts = 2.5 grams
2/3 cup cooked broccoli = 3.1 grams
6-8 cooked Brussels sprouts = 4.2 grams
⅔ cup cooked peas = 5.4 grams
1 raw bell pepper = 1.2 grams
1 large baked potato = 3.9 grams

Calcium and iron are two other nutritional concerns. The consumption of animal products creates an acidic condition in the blood that can draw calcium from the bones. The calcium in leafy green vegetables and legumes, along with tofu, parsley, sesame seeds, hijiki and wakame, is utilized much more readily than that found in meat and dairy products. Leafy greens and beans are a good source of iron, as well, and getting an adequate amount of vitamin C can help increase iron absorption.

The RDA of calcium for adults is 800 milligrams (and some researchers consider this too be too high). Vegetarians can use:

1 cup cooked greens (collards, kale, turnip greens, spinach) = 200-300 mg.
1 cup cooked beans = 100 mg
2 slices tofu = 305 mg
2 cups soy milk = 95 mg
2 Tbsp. arame (sea vegetable) = 34 mg.

The RDA of iron for women is 18 mg. and for men 10 mg. Good sources in a vegetarian diet are:

1 cup cooked greens (collards, kale, turnip greens, spinach) = 1-2 mg
1 cup cooked beans = 4-6 mg
1 cup soy milk or ¼ lb. tofu = 2 mg
2 Tbsp. arame (sea vegetable) = .5 mg.

One nutrient that you need to supplement if you eat no animal products at all is vitamin B12. If you go a long time without it, you risk damage to your nervous system. The RDA is about 3 micrograms (mcg.) per day. If you supplement orally, taking 25 mcg. twice a week is about right, as not all of it will be absorbed and any excess will be eliminated. Some vegetarian foods, like nutritional yeast and textured vegetable protein, have vitamin B12 added to them. Tempeh is not a reliable source.

Recently much has appeared in the news about the need for fiber in your diet. Dietary fiber is more than the "roughage" of celery and bran flakes that we think of; it also includes soluble fibers, like gums and the pectins found in fruit and agar agar. These are actually smooth fibers. Nutritional research has discovered the importance of fiber as a cleanser in the colon. It keeps the moisture content of the colon balanced so that digested material will move along quickly and not increase the chance of absorption of toxic wastes that the body is trying to eliminate. A natural foods diet offers a much greater variety of fiber sources than an animal protein diet. Some of the best sources are oats, prunes, green peas and corn. Along with the carbohydrate foods that everyone associates with fiber, vegetable protein foods are also good sources of fiber. One cup of beans has as much dietary fiber as ⅔ cup of oat bran but is more fun to eat.

So tomorrow, try a hearty breakfast based on fruit and grains. Blueberry pancakes can start the day off much better for you than a heart-threatening breakfast of bacon and eggs. Or a dinner based on a delicious bean casserole instead of pork chops can be as good to eat as it is for you.

The Natural Foods Pantry

Many of the foods you'll eat more of on a natural foods diet are already familiar, such as rice, wheat flour, beans and lots of fruits and vegetables. With these recipes you have some interesting new ways to use these ingredients. There are other beans, grains and vegetables that may be new to you, but are so delicious and nutritious that they deserve your consideration, like aduki beans, quinoa and sea vegetables.

Grains

The majority of the world's population eats a diet based on whole grains. They are the most economical and nutritious food available. Grains supply both protein for body building and carbohydrates for the strong and vital kind of energy that the body needs to run on. They are also good sources of dietary fiber, B vitamins, vitamin E, zinc, iron and magnesium. Refining grains strips away much of the fiber, vitamins and minerals that make these foods so valuable in a good diet. The rich B vitamin and phosphorus content helps promote mental clarity. Also, whole grains (with the exception of wheat) can help reduce fat in the body.

When you cook whole grains, add a pinch of sea salt to the cooking water to break down the cellulose and make the grain more digestible. Be sure to chew grains well. Although grains are acid-forming (except for millet), they will break down as alkaline in the body if they are chewed thoroughly; digestion begins in the mouth. Oriental medicine is based on the belief that each organ has a grain that is especially suitable for nourishing its force. Rice is recommended for the lungs, buckwheat and beans (particularly aduki) for the kidneys, yellow millet for the spleen, red (glutinous) millet for the heart and wheat for the liver.

Brown rice is considered by macrobiotics to be the most balanced and evolved cereal grain. It is rich in B vitamins and trace minerals and is particularly soothing to the nervous system and brain. It is often avoided by the calorie-conscious, yet a half cup of cooked rice contains only 100 calories. Brown rice is considered the easiest grain to digest and good for people with allergies. Phytin acid is found in the germ of brown rice and is said to help expel poisons from the body.

There are several varieties of brown rice to choose from. Short grain is the smallest, the hardiest, contains the most minerals, is lower in protein and high in gluten. It is particularly emphasized for the winter months because of its compact structure which creates more energy, warmth and vitality. Medium grain is a little larger. When you cook it, it becomes moister and softer than short grain. The lightest variety is long grain. It is best eaten in the summer months and is lighter in the stomach than other varieties. Sweet brown rice is most glutinous, contains more protein and is the easiest to digest. It's the variety used to make "mochi" (cakes or squares formed from pounded cooked sweet rice). It is recommended for babies, children and increasing the milk flow in nursing mothers. Basmati rice (which is now available in white or brown varieties and is often used in Indian cooking) has a subtley sweet aroma, which makes it a nice change from traditional varieties. Wild rice is the only grain native to North America. Compared to refined white rice, it has twice as much protein, six times the iron and 20 times the vitamin B-2. In addition it contains lysine, an amino acid that most grains lack.

If you buy brown rice from bulk bins at a health food store, rinse and inspect it for small stones before cooking. The standard recipe for cooking brown rice is one cup of rice to one and a fourth cups water, simmering slowly for about 30 minutes. Check to see if the water has been absorbed; if not, continue cooking slowly for up to 15 minutes longer. Add more liquid if necessary to make rice tender. Adding the rice to the water before boiling will make the rice softer. Pressure cooking is recommended as the best way to prepare whole grains and brown rice. It brings out the natural sweetness of the rice and makes it more digestible. To pressure cook, combine 2 cups of water and 1½ cups rice for approximately 30 minutes. Again, a pinch of sea salt per cup of rice will help soften the grain during the cooking process.

Barley has been used by Western cultures for centuries, best known as an addition to soups. Next to rice, barley is the easiest grain to digest and is therefore good for sick people. It is said to stimulate the liver and lymphatic system, enhancing the discharge of poisonous wastes from the body. Hato mugi barley is a specific strain shown to reduce tumors and fats in the body.

Pearled barley (as opposed to the smaller and more compact "pearl" barley) has been refined of its protein, vitamins and minerals, but is easy to digest. Hulled barley is a good choice as it still retains a fair amount of its original nutritional value. Besides its use in soups, barley makes an excellent addition to stuffing and casseroles and barley flour can be added to breads, muffins and crackers. It can also be roasted and boiled to make barley tea.

Buckwheat is the hardiest of all the cereal grains. It is especially high in vitamin E, calcium and other minerals and is extremely warming to the body. It provides reservoirs of stamina and energy in the winter. Said to be beneficial to the kidneys it's also a good blood builder. It's actually a fruit, but nutritionally is more similar to a grain. The kernels are called groats and roasted kernels are called kasha. The Japanese are very fond of buckwheat noodles called soba. Buckwheat makes a good breakfast cereal; buckwheat flour is a tasty addition to baked goods.

Corn is a grain basic to Latin American cooking, as well as a staple in the good old-fashioned corn bread enjoyed on a daily basis by many Southerners. It's the only common grain that contains vitamin A, as well as protein, B vitamins, calcium, iron and other minerals. Corn is cooling in the summer and helps build strong blood. It is said to be strengthening to the heart and circulatory system. Nutritionally it is the least complete grain and is best eaten with a variety of other foods, including beans. Corn comes in many varieties, from the sweet corn-on-the-cob in summer to dent corn from which corn meal is made. Blue corn, an Indian corn, makes delicious corn chips and tortillas. Corn pasta is available as an alternative to wheat pasta. Corn is very versatile in a natural foods diet as it can be used either as a starchy vegetable or a grain.

The use of *millet* goes back further than any other cereal grain. It lends itself to many recipes, from breakfast cereal and side dishes to puddings and baked goods. It is especially good for people with gluten allergies. Millet is very high in protein, minerals, lecithin and B vitamins. Millet is said to be good for the spleen, stomach and pancreas. Because it is the only grain that cooks up alkaline, it is good for people with acidosis.

Oats are a staple in the British Isles where a hot bowl of oatmeal starts the day. Besides being a good source of protein, B and E vitamins and minerals, oats are an excellent source of dietary fiber and can help reduce blood cholesterol. Oats, more than other grains, can stabilize glucose levels in the blood, which is especially significant for diabetics. They are also good for people with slow thyroids. They contain the highest percentage of fat of any grain, imparting warmth and stamina to the body. Most of us are familiar with the use of oats in baked goods, but they can also be added to main dishes like stews and casseroles. Whole oat groats are preferred for everyday use. They are hulled, take longer to prepare and cook up creamy. Steel-cut oats are hulled, scoured, steamed and coarsely cut with steel blades. Because they are mechanically split, they have less vitality than whole oats. Rolled oats have been steamed, then passed through rollers which flatten them into flakes. They are the quickest cooking. Products containing oat bran are becoming increasingly popular due to its cholesterol reducing ability.

Rye evokes images of fat, round, dark loaves of delicious bread so popular in northern Europe. It is similar to whole wheat in nutritional value, but is higher in the amino acid lysine than any other grain. It is a good source of protein, B vitamins, vitamin E, iron and phosphorus. Rye, along with wheat, provides energy, endurance and enhances muscle strength. Its low gluten content makes it a good grain for people allergic to wheat. Although you can cook whole rye like rice, it's easier to digest in flour, cereal flakes or a cracked form, similar to bulghur wheat.

Whole wheat is the most popular grain in this country. If the entire grain is used, it provides a good source of protein, B and E vitamins, essential fatty acids, iron, fiber and important trace minerals. Whole wheat is said to be beneficial to the liver. Wheat bran is the richest source of insoluable fiber which helps to prevent constipation, diverticulosis, and colon and rectal cancer. It is suggested the average adult needs 2 Tbsp. of bran a day.

Wheat comes in several varieties. Hard wheat is used for making bread because of its high gluten content. Soft winter wheat contains more carbohydrates and is used mostly in pastries and for mixing with harder flours. Spring wheat may be "hard" or "soft". Whole wheat pastry flour comes from spring wheat that is low in gluten and is used for making crackers and pastries. Durum is a low gluten variety used for pasta, one of the most nutritious "fast foods". Many people still think of pasta as fattening, although it is lower in calories than a comparable amount of potatoes or rice. Besides the many varieties of Italian pastas you can find in supermarkets, try vegetable pastas made from wheat flour and vegetable paste and udon, a Japanese whole wheat noodle. Whole wheat berries can be cooked like brown rice and eaten alone or mixed with other grains. Cracked wheat that has been partially boiled, dried and ground is called bulghur, a popular Middle Eastern dish. It can be prepared by just adding water and soaking, to make a sandwich filling or grain salad. Couscous is another Middle Eastern favorite made from cracked semolina wheat that can be used as a side dish or sweetened for breakfast or dessert. Triticale is a cross between wheat and rye and makes good bread.

There are regional, traditional grains that have been in existence for centuries that are just appearing in natural foods markets. *Amaranth* was the sacred grain of the Aztecs. It is higher in protein than wheat or corn, supplying all the essential amino acids to make it a complete protein. It is a good source of vitamin C, unlike most grains, and provides a good source of iron and calcium. Because it is gluten-free, it's a good grain for people with allergies to wheat. You can toast it to use in a side dish with other grains. *Quinoa* (pronounced keen-wa) was a staple of the Inca Indians. Like amaranth it is a complete protein and rich in fatty acids, vitamins and minerals. It lacks gluten, an advantage for those with allergies to gluten and wheat. Quinoa is very digestible and light, making it an ideal grain for summertime meals. It cooks up in fifteen minutes and increases almost five times its size. Be sure to rinse quinoa before cooking to remove a bitter resin that coats the seeds. It makes a delicious grain salad or stuffing. Pastas are now available that are made both from amaranth and quinoa.

Kamut (Pronounced Ka-moot) is an ancient Egyptian wheat, originally grown in the Valley of the Nile, and related to modern durum wheats. The name itself was the word for wheat in the days of the pharoahs. Kamut has a unique, nutty flavor, and is higher in protein than durum or bread wheats. It is also rich in lipids and minerals. Because it is less closely related to the bread wheats, some people allergic to those wheats may not be allergic to kamut. Kamut is being grown in Montana and is available as a whole grain, pasta, or flour.

Teff, an Ethiopian grain, is among the latest ancient grains being harvested in the U.S. It is considered the smallest grain in the world. Teff is said to contain more fiber-rich germ and bran than any other grain, and to have 17 times the calcium of whole wheat or barley. Extremely versatile, teff can be eaten cooked or uncooked. Uncooked, teff can be eaten as a plain cereal, added to breads, and other baked goods. It can be cooked in stews, soups, casseroles, gravies, puddings, and pies. When substituting teff for other nuts, seeds, grains, or in baked good recipes, use less teff. For example, if replacing one cup of sesame seeds, use ½ cup of teff.

Spelt, a light brown grain that is larger than wheat, originated in southeast Asia. Spelt is rich in protein, carbohydrates, vitamins and iron. It is not a hybrid like wheat and is good for those allergic to wheat. Because of its heartiness, spelt takes about 30 to 40 minutes to cook.

Beans

Beans are a perfect match for whole grains in a natural foods diet, both for nutrition and taste. One cup of beans a day can lower cholesterol as effectively as ⅔ cup of oat bran. The lack of certain amino acids in grains is made up for by their abundance in beans. Beans supply the body with concentrated amounts of protein and energy. They contain protease inhibitors (as do by-products of soybeans such as tofu and miso) which research indicates may prevent cancer of the stomach, digestive tract and esophagus. Beans are also a good source of calcium in a vegetarian diet, along with fiber, vitamin E, phosphorus and potassium. The aduki bean is said to be good for the kidneys. Green peas are good for the stomach; whole navy and lima beans contain less oil and are good for liver problems. Black beans are said to be good for the sexual organs and are claimed to enhance male sexual virility. Healthy individuals should limit their intake of cooked legumes to one cup per day so their protein intake does not become excessive.

If you've had trouble digesting beans properly in the past, don't despair. There are ways to cook beans that makes them easy to eat. Soak your beans before cooking them (which also reduces cooking time) and add a bay leaf, a teaspoon of kelp or a strip of kombu while cooking. To reduce cooking time you can bring your beans to a boil for a few minutes and then let them sit for one hour. Sort and rinse beans well before cooking. The mechanical sorting processes don't always remove bean-size stones and can't discriminate between shriveled beans and whole ones.

A pressure cooker helps you eat a variety of beans on a regular basis. A four quart cooker is adequate for a family of four and a six quart model is handy if you like making several meals worth of beans at a time and freezing them. Besides making your beans softer and more digestible, a pressure cooker greatly reduces cooking time. Pinto beans might take as long as 2½ hours to cook while simmering in a covered pot, but can be cooked in an hour in a pressure cooker. See the cooking chart for beans and grains on the facing page. The only beans I don't advise cooking in a pressure cooker are lentils and split peas. They tend to clog the pressure vent. Follow the instructions that come with your pressure cooker.

Pinto beans are a natural in south-of-the-border recipes. *White beans*, such as navy or great northerns, are the basic ingredients for Boston baked beans. *Black beans* show up in Creole and Brazilian cuisine. *Garbanzos* star in Middle Eastern favorites such as falafel. *Black-eyed peas* go hand in hand with cornbread in the South. *Lentils and split peas* make delicious soups. *Mung and adzuki beans* are Oriental favorites.

Cooking Beans and Grains

Per 1 cup beans (presoaked 6-8 hours)

Bean	Water	Cooking Time*
Aduki	3 cups	45-60 min./8 min.
Black	4 cups	2 hrs./30-35 min.
Garbanzo (Chick-pea)	4 cups	3 hrs./30-40 min.
Great Northern	3½ cups	2 hrs./30 min.
Kidney	3 cups	simmer only 45 min.
Lima	3 cups	2 hrs./30 min.
Lentil*	2 cups	1½ hrs./25 min.
Navy	3 cups	2 hrs./15-20 min.
Red	3 cups	4 hrs./1 hr.
Pinto	3 cups	2 hrs./35-40 min.
Soy	3 cups	pressure cook only 45 min./1 hr.
Split Pea*	3 cups	simmer only 1 hr.

Simmer/Pressure Cook

Per 1 cup grains:

Grain	Water	Cooking Time
Barley	3 cups	1-1¼ hrs.
Brown Rice	1¼ to 1½ cups	40 min.
Buckwheat	2 cups	15-20 min.
Bulghur	2 cups	15 min.
Cornmeal	4 cups	20-25 min.
Couscous	2 cups	1 min.
Millet	2½ cups	15-20 min.
Rolled oats	3 cups	10 min.
Wheat Berries	3 cups	2 hrs.

*Needs no presoaking

Soy Foods

Soybeans are the elite of the legumes. These highly nutritious beans provide complete protein. The presence of lecithin in soybeans can lower serum cholesterol and help reduce the risk of heart disease. As people become more aware of the health risks from eating meat and the environmental problems caused by large-scale animal husbandry, soybeans will become increasingly important as a source of high quality protein.

Tofu, or bean curd as it's known in the Orient, is a bland, custard-like product made by curdling soymilk. The curds are then pressed to form either a soft, medium firm or firm block. It can be sliced or crumbled and lends itself to an incredible array of uses in everything from appetizers to desserts. Tofu is one of the most nutritious and versatile protein foods in the world and is economical as well.

Like all soy products tofu is cholesterol free and contains lecithin and linoleic acid which help break down cholesterol. It's a perfect low calorie protein source for dieters, as a 3 oz. serving of tofu contains only 67.5 calories compared to 3 oz. of cottage cheese with 127 calories. Although a greater percentage of tofu's calories are from fat than other beans and grains (49% as compared to 37% from plain soybeans, 3-4% from other beans and 4-5% from rice or wheat), it is less than most animal products (64% for lean ground beef, 63% for tuna, 65% from eggs and 55% for mozzarella cheese). Its digestibility makes it an ideal food for older babies and the elderly. Tofu is also a good source of calcium.

Tofu is now in the produce sections of supermarkets as well as oriental markets and natural food stores. It's usually sold prepackaged in a plastic tub covered with water, in a vacuum packed plastic bag, in bulk or in aseptic packaging that will keep it fresh for up to one year if unopened. Store bulk tofu in the refrigerator in cold water that should be changed daily, so the tofu will stay fresh and keep for about a week. It should be white in color and barely have any smell to it. A slightly sour smell is okay, but if you've purchased some that smells very sour, return it to your grocer. You can often find both soft tofu, which is ideal for blending into dips, dressings and desserts, and firm tofu for dishes where you want the tofu to hold its form.

Tofu may be frozen, which completely changes its texture. When thawed it becomes spongy and chewy. It will soak up marinades and sauces more readily than plain tofu. It can be frozen right in its package. To thaw, leave it out at room temperature; a pound of frozen tofu will be ready to use after a few hours. If you're in a hurry, pour boiling water over it. Squeeze out the excess moisture from thawed tofu before using.

Because tofu will absorb the flavor of whatever it's cooked with, there are few foods as versatile. For a low cholesterol breakfast, tofu can be used to replace eggs. Crumbled or cubed tofu can be sauteed with vegetables and sprinkled with tumeric to resemble the color of eggs. An eggless salad can be made by mashing tofu and adding tofu mayonnaise, minced vegetables and tumeric. Try a delicious tofu dip at your next party. As an entree, tofu makes great meatless meals. As a dessert, tofu makes an unbelievable cheese cake, pudding and much more. Tofu is an ingredient in a number of ready-to-eat items now available in natural food stores, such as tofu hot dogs, burgers and sausage, mayonnaise, salad dressings and dips, tofu ice cream and frozen tofu dinner entrees such as manicotti, enchiladas and lasagne. If you've tried tofu before and didn't really like it, experiment with some of the many tempting ways this food can be used.

Tempeh is a fermented soybean cake made by natural culturing, similar to that used to make cheese, yogurt and sourdough. It originated in Indonesia where it is the main protein source for millions of people. Tempeh is gaining in popularity in this country as more people become aware of its delicious nutty taste, meaty texture, nutritional benefits and economical price.

Tempeh has the highest quality protein of all the soyfoods, as it contains most of the whole bean. Fresh soy tempeh has nearly as much protein (18%) per serving as beef (20%) or chicken (21%) and more than hamburger, eggs and milk (all at 13%). It is a high fiber food, free of cholesterol and contains natural antibiotics that safeguard the intestinal tract. Tempeh is also very digestible.

It has a nutty flavor that resembles chicken or veal. Tempeh can be made from other beans, grains and seeds and some varieties mix in vegetables and sea vegetables. Virtually any recipe that calls for meat could substitute tempeh. Always steam or cook your tempeh for 20 minutes before eating or preparing by a quick-cooking method such as sauteing - never eat raw tempeh. You can add tempeh to salads, pasta, casseroles, spaghetti sauce, chili, stews, soups, enchiladas, burritos, tacos and sandwich spreads. In natural food stores you can find ready-to-eat burgers, tempeh salads, vegetarian chili, tempeh bacon and strami.

Miso (me-so) is a creamy paste made from fermented soybeans and sea salt. It has been a favorite of the Japanese for centuries, who use it as a flavoring, a digestive aid and a health tonic. It is a savory, high-protein seasoning and comes in a range of flavors, colors, textures and aromas. In Japan, people start their day with a cup of miso soup, because its alkalizing effect wakes up the mind and body. Miso is low in calories and fat.

Because it is a cultured food, miso is rich in lactic acid and enzymes which play a vital role in digestion. Miso is also said to discharge radioactive strontium 90 from the body, prevent radiation sickness, dissolve and discharge cholesterol, assist in neutralizing the effects of environmental pollution and replenish healthy bacteria destroyed by antibiotics. Japan's National Cancer Center found that those people who eat miso soup daily are 33% less likely to contract cancer than those who don't.

Naturally aged, organic, unpasturized miso is considered the best quality. It should be kept refrigerated. There are light misos; mellow, sweet and white. These varieties are high in carbohydrates and "koji", a bacterial mold high in enzymes, and low in salt. The dark misos, red, soybean and barley are higher in salt, protein and fatty acids and low in koji. They are best suited for winter cooking. In addition to soup, miso is delicious in dressings, sauces, marinades, gravies, as a seasoning for beans and can be used as a substitute for bouillon and butter in some recipes. Never boil miso as this destroys valuable enzymes. Dissolve it first in a small amount of water or stock and add to a recipe shortly before serving.

The growing number of people with an allergy to dairy products is creating a demand for soy milk, soy cheese and soy yogurt. *Soy milk* is made from grinding soaked soy beans into a paste, cooking them in water and then straining, leaving a rich milky liquid. Like other soy foods, soy milk is cholesterol and lactose free. It is lower in fat than dairy milk but can be substituted in any recipe in which you could use skim milk. It's the base for tofu, soy yogurt, soy ice cream and whipped cream. Commercially prepared soymilk is available in natural food stores, either fresh in the dairy case or in asceptic cartons that will keep unrefrigerated for about twelve months. Soy milk is not recommended for very young babies. It doesn't have the right balance of casein, milk sugars, and other carbohydrates to be properly assimilated by an infant.

Soy cheeses are lactose and cholesterol-free. Soft soy cheese is made from tofu, whipped to a consistency of cream cheese. Most firmer cheeses are made with a milk protein called casein, although new varieties are available without it. Soy yogurt can be cultured at home and is now available in several commercial varieties.

You should also be aware of the uses of flour, grits and powder ground from whole soy beans. *Soy flour* has a nutty flavor from roasting the beans before they are ground. You can substitute ¼ cup of soy flour for wheat flour in a recipe to increase the nutritional value of home baked bread. *Soy grits* are a great addition to cooked grains; use two parts water to one part grits. Be sure to refrigerate soy flour and grits to reduce rancidity of the oils they contain. *Soy powder* has been cooked and most of the fat removed, so it makes a good instant soy milk with a low fat content. Because it contains so little oil, it will keep without refrigeration. It is best used in baking and cooking.

If you make your own soy milk at home, you may wonder what to do with the pulp that remains after the milk is strained. This *soy "pulp" or okara* is a primary ingredient in soy "sausage" and can be used in casseroles, cookies and croquettes. It enhances the moisture and texture of baked goods and can be dried and used in granola or to replace bread crumbs as a topping for casseroles.

Vegetables and Fruits

When you eat less meat and fewer high calorie desserts, fresh produce begins to play a greater role in providing the necessary ingredients for a balanced diet in ways that might surprise you.

The cruciferous vegetables such as broccoli, carrots, cabbage, green beans and cauliflower are high in fiber and are seen as protective foods in preventing cancer. They contain indoles, which researchers believe may enhance their protective factor. Broccoli stems actually contain more fiber than the flowers, so be sure to use them. Dr. Richard Peto of Britain's Imperial Cancer Research discovered that the beta-carotene form of vitamin A found in vegetables is more effective in reducing the risk of cancer than the preformed vitamin A found in eggs, dairy products and some meats. Our bodies convert the beta-carotene in fruits (such as peaches, apricots and watermelon) and dark, green leafy and deep yellow vegetables (such as winter squash and carrots) to vitamin A in the body. Shiitake mushrooms, delicious, large, dried mushrooms from Japan, are said to have anti-viral properties and are stimulating to the immune system.

Dark, green leafy vegetables, such as kale, collards, mustard greens, turnip and radish greens and broccoli, should be included in the diet every day. They are seen as protective foods because they are a rich source of chlorophyll, vitamin A, C, and E, and help build healthy blood. They also offer substantial amounts of iron, potassium, thiamin, riboflavin and calcium. Root vegetables such as parsnips, turnips, rutabagas and Jerusalem artichokes (the root of a member of the sunflower family) are a good source of vitamin C and provide calcium, potassium and riboflavin. Green beans, especially string beans assist the body in producing insulin and are a good source of vitamins A and C. Cook green beans uncut to preserve nutrients and cut stems after cooking. Asparagus is another good source of vitamin A. It is best not to eat it raw as it contains certain toxins that are neutralized if the asparagus is simmered for 8 to 12 minutes. Kale, watercress and sorrel are among the richest sources of the anti-aging nutrients, such as vitamin C, silicon and sulphur. Macrobiotic theory recommends using tomatoes, spinach, beet greens and swiss chard sparingly because they contain oxalic acid, which inhibits the absorption of calcium, zinc and magnesium. Be sure to save your steaming or blanching water as many of the vegetables' nutrients will otherwise be poured down the drain. Use this water for tea, soup stock or gravies.

Besides a high vitamin and mineral content, the percentage of calories from protein these vegetables contain ranges from 40% to 50%. This rivals most beans and is higher than grains, nuts and seeds. If you're looking for the best protein ratio versus the amount of calories you consume, these nutritious vegetables can help you meet your needs. Dairy foods have been touted as the prime sources of calcium, yet leafy green vegetables, beans, some nuts and seeds and seaweeds contain more calcium than similar amounts of cow's milk.

Along with beans, many fruits and vegetables are rich sources of iron. If you take a piece of lean steak big enough to provide you with 100 calories and compare it to either 100 calories worth of spinach, beet or mustard greens, kale, bell peppers, tomatoes, strawberries or dried apricots, the fruits and vegetables would come out on top. Since we're only comparing calories in this instance, you'll need to eat a greater "volume" of fruits and vegetables to get 100 calories than you would of that steak. But when you consider the variety of ways you can work these foods into your diet and their low cost, it's not hard to utilize their tremendous nutritional punch.

Sea Vegetables

For centuries, sea vegetables have been used as a nutritious staple in the diets of people who live by the sea such as the Japanese, Irish, Scotch, Russians and the South Pacific Islanders. Some 25% of all food consumed in Japan consists of sea vegetables in some fashion. In American colonial times a seaweed called dulse was eaten widely in New England and even served in pubs much like chips and beer nuts are today. Most of us today are eating sea vegetables as standard ingredients in cheese, ice cream, baked goods and some processed foods. In a healthy diet, there should be a balance of land and sea vegetables. Macrobiotic theory recommends that 2 tablespoons of sea vegetables be eaten daily.

There is concern over sea vegetables being contaminated from polluted ocean waters. However, some harvesters (such as off the coast of Maine) have tested their sea vegetables and found them to be below the FDA threshold for heavy metals and other contaminants. If sea vegetables contain toxic metals, researchers hope to establish whether or not they are simply carried through the body, since sea vegetables do bond with those substances and remove them.

As knowledge of the tremendous nutritional value of sea vegetables increases, they are becoming more available. Sea vegetables are a rich source of vitamin A, E, all the B vitamins (even B12 in some cases), iron, calcium and other minerals, as well as protein. They are the only source of iodine outside of fish. Sea vegetables are very important in assisting the proper functioning of the thyroid gland, which in turn affects the body's metabolic processes. They appear to be body cleansers, ridding the system of fats and other impurities and protecting against infection and disease. Research at McGill University in Canada has shown that the darker sea vegetables can remove radioactive strontium-90 from the body.

Agar-agar is used for its jelling properties and can be substituted for gelatin in desserts, jellies, preserves, aspics and fillings. Try the jellied salads or dessert recipes included in the book. It is available in flakes, powder, strands or bars called kanten. It will set adequately at room temperature or more quickly with refrigeration. In making aspics or savories it is best to use lemon juice (citric acid), apple cider vinegar or malt vinegar (malic acid). Agar will not set in the presence of acetic acid, found in wine and distilled vinegars. It also will not set with the high proportion of oxalic acid found in spinach, chocolate and rhubarb. For these foods, Irish moss must be substituted. It is not necessary to soak agar flakes or powder in cold water prior to use. Kanten bars, however, should be broken into pieces, washed, wrung out and soaked in water for 30 minutes. The agar is then added to liquid, brought to a boil and stirred until completely dissolved, around 8 minutes. Agar is rich in iron, calcium, phosphorus, iodine and vitamins A, C, and K. While the calorie count is negligible, agar adds fiberous bulk to the diet. It can also be used as a mild laxative. It has been shown to work like pectin, bonding with toxic metals such as lead, and radionuclides, to carry them out of the body.

Arame is a brown sea vegetable with a sweet, delicate taste that can be sautéed with tofu or root vegetables. It can add a shrimp-like taste to soups, salads and curries. Soak it for five minutes before using; one ounce expands to two cups after soaking. Arame is high in complex carbohydrates, fiber, iron, calcium, niacin and iodine. Traditionally, it has been used to treat female disorders and is said to help reduce blood pressure.

Dulse may be the most suited to American tastes. It can be added raw to salads, soups, fritters, mashed potatoes and breads. It comes in powdered form and can be used as a condiment. The raw strands can also be dry roasted in a skillet, then ground into powder and sprinkled on casseroles, salads, soups, and grains, etc. Dulse is very high in protein and has the highest concentration of iron of all the sea vegetables.

Hijiki (or hiziki) is a brown seaweed with a delicious nut-like flavor and crisp texture that can be added to noodles, salads, casseroles, quiches, cooked rice, stews and soups. It needs to be well rinsed (three to four times) and sautéed in oil to release the oil-soluable vitamins (E and carotene) it contains. Hijiki expands to five times its original volume when soaked. This sea vegetable deserves an important place in the diet. It contains more calcium than *any* other food source. One tablespoon of hijiki contains as much calcium as a glass of milk. It contains over 10 times more calcium than a comparable volume of milk, cheese or other dairy food! Hijiki is recommended for purifying the blood, producing beautiful hair and strengthening the intestines.

Kombu is a brown sea vegetable grown off the coast of Maine, as well as Japan. It has a sweet taste and contains glutamic acid, a natural flavor enhancer that works even better than MSG. It has a variety of uses, as an addition to beans, grains and root vegetables, condiments, candies, snacks, pickles and teas. A strip placed on the bottom of a pot of beans or rice will keep them from sticking. It also helps make beans more digestible and speeds up their cooking time. Soak kombu for three to five minutes before using or rinse thoroughly under cold water and pat dry with a paper towel. Kombu contains almost all the elements essential for bodily metabolism and was found by McGill University to help reduce the effects of radiation poisoning. It is said to provide therapeutic protection against degenerative disease.

Nori is sold in sheets and is popular today because of its use in making sushi. Instead of soaking or rinsing, nori is usually toasted over low heat to improve its digestibility. It can also be baked in a slow oven for four or five minutes, then crushed into a powder and used as a condiment. Of all the sea vegetables, nori is the highest in protein and vitamin A (two to four times as much as carrots, 10 times that in bell peppers and 50 times as much as tomatoes), and vitamins B and C. It is also high in B-12. Nori has been shown to reduce high serum cholesterol levels.

Wakame is a brown seaweed like kombu and hijiki and is the most widely consumed of all the sea vegetables. It's a popular addition to miso soup and can be used with vegetable dishes, cold salads and condiments. Soak it for just a few minutes before using or roast in a slow oven and grind it with nuts or seeds. High in calcium, protein, vitamins and minerals, it is claimed by some to detoxify the body and strengthen the body's immune system.

Fruits

Fruit in the diet is a very important source of vitamins, minerals, fiber, little if any fat (except avocadoes, which are high in fat) or sodium and no cholesterol. Fruits have a high percentage of cellulose (fiber) providing bulk for digestion. This is important for keeping the colon clean and safeguarding against colon disorders and cancer. Fruits are very important in assisting the crucial elimination channels of the body. They support the breakdown of blood cells and the riddance of waste matter. Cooling to the body, they are emphasized in the diet during the hot summer months and during their season of harvest. Except for cranberries, prunes and plums they are alkalizing to the body. It is suggested that because fruit is expansive, if too much is consumed, you might experience light-headedness and a lack of ability to concentrate, along with a weakening of the intestines. People with low blood sugar should avoid dates and grapes.

Citrus fruits, cantaloupes and strawberries are important sources of vitamin C in the diet, while fat-rich fruits such as olives and avocadoes provide unsaturated fatty acids. Olives are especially rich in lecithin, which helps to keep cholesterol levels down. The high vitamin C content of many fruits make them possible anti-cancer foods. The food combining of fruits is very important. Melons should be eaten alone because they digest quickly. Sweet fruits and proteins should never be combined together. Nuts and seeds or milk products can be used with the acid (oranges, lemons, grapefruit, pineapple, tomato, strawberries, tangerines) and sub-acid fruits (apple, grape, pears, blueberries, peaches, plums, nectarines and figs).

Sprouts

Sprouts are a great way to keep fresh, live pesticide-free food growing at home, particularly in the winter. They are easy to grow, very economical and loaded with vitamins A and C, as well as protein. Alfalfa sprouts are the most popular, available ready-to-eat from your supermarket. Other beans and seeds that you can sprout are wheat or rye berries, unhulled buckwheat, sunflower and sesame seeds, radish seeds, mung and soy beans, lentils and garbanzo beans. They can replace the lettuce in sandwiches, be added to any salad or lightly sautéed with other vegetables.

Periodic rinsing and draining of the seeds is what encourages the growth of sprouts. The chart below shows the amount of seeds to use in a quart jar, one of the easiest containers for sprouting. At natural food stores you can buy screened jar lids that are made specially for the job. You can also take cheese cloth or rust-proof metal screen (fine enough to keep your seeds from falling through) and use thick rubber bands or canning jar rings to hold the material in place. Don't sprout seeds that are sold for garden use, as they're coated with fungicide.

To start your sprouts, measure out seeds into the jar and fill with about three times as much warm water. Soak overnight and drain the next morning. The soaking liquid contains a certain amount of nutrients, so you may want to save it for soup stock or even watering your plants. Rinse your sprouts twice a day in cool water (more often in hot weather to keep them from molding). Prop up your sprout jar at an inverted slant in your dish drainer or a bowl, out of direct sunlight. This way the seeds will drain well and can be spread out around the sides of the jar to encourage better growth. You can cover the jar with a towel to keep out light until the sprouts are almost done. Toward the end of the growing cycle, the loose seed hulls will float to the top of the jar when filled with rinse water, making them easy to pour out the top. You can find out when your sprouts have reached their peak flavor by giving them an occasional taste test. The larger sprouts, particularly soybean sprouts, are often better and easier to digest after being steamed for several minutes. Refrigerate your finished sprouts, rinsing them occasionally to keep them fresh.

For one quart of sprouts:

Seed	Start with	Time to grow
Alfalfa	2 Tbsp.	4-5 days
Garbanzo	¾ cup	4 days
Lentil	½ cup	3-4 days
Mung Bean	½ cup	3-4 days
Radish	¼ cup	4 days
Soybean	1 cup	4 days
Sunflower	2 cups	2-3 days
Wheat Berry	1 cup	3-5 days

Sweeteners

Since our childhood days we've been warned that we'd have problems with tooth decay if we ate too much sugar. Now reports are coming out that link excess sugar consumption to diabetes, high blood pressure, and heart disease, as well as hyperactivity in children. What is it about sugar that makes it such a problem in our diet?

Sugar doesn't supply the body with anything nutritionally except calories. We've developed such a sweet tooth that food manufacturers have added it to every conceivable processed food, so we consume much more of it than we realize. Other sweeteners such as honey, barley malt, and of course, molasses, have enough flavor that it's more difficult to eat large quantities of them. Claims have been made that other sweeteners are preferable to sugar because of the vitamins and minerals they contain. However, these nutrients appear in such small quantities that they can be considered negligible. Molasses does contain appreciable amounts of iron, but not any more for the amount of calories it contains than strawberries. Recent studies at Tufts University suggest that glucose sugar (white sugar) may actually improve absorption of calcium by the intestine, so the controversy marches on. Not many of us would want to give up tasty sweet treats forever, but the key is definitely moderation and awareness of the hidden sweeteners in our foods.

Another consideration with sweeteners is the pesticide problem. Most of the white sugar we consume has been grown with pesticides. Pesticide residues also appear in honey, so it's wise to look for organic brands. A few other sweeteners, like barley malt syrup and brown rice syrup (yinnie), are products more closely associated with natural foods and have a greater chance of being free of contaminates.

In my own personal cooking I prefer to use barley malt and brown rice syrup. They are certainly more expensive than many of the other sweeteners but to me are worth the price. Because they are made from sprouted grains, they appear to be absorbed more slowly into the bloodstream and don't seem to have the effect on the blood sugar level that sugar, honey, corn syrup and the other sweeteners do. I've provided recipes using these sweeteners so you can get an idea of how you can incorporate them into your diet.

Avoid giving honey to babies under one year old. It may contain botulism spores that young digestive systems cannot tolerate.

Oils

High quality oils combined with high quality protein create the cell structure on which the energy from carbohydrates operate. Some vitamins, such as A and D, need oil to dissolve in so they can be utilized by the body. The beneficial aspects of oil in our food is so easily destroyed by commercial processing and improper storage that these factors are key considerations in choosing which oils to use.

Oils, as with sweeteners, often slip into our diet unnoticed and the high concentration of calories they provide are often blamed on the wrong food. Many of us avoid potatoes, baked goods and pastas because we think they're fattening when it's actually the gravy, sour cream, shortening and butter that are the calorie culprits. Yet oil is such an essential in our diet we need to retrain ourselves in its use.

In many kitchens butter and margarine are being replaced by oils for every day cooking. Butter contains cholesterol, which many people are avoiding. Because pesticides are always more concentrated in oils the higher up in the food chain they are found, the pesticides found in cattle feed end up in greater quantities in your butter than in vegetable oil sources. The presence of antibiotics in butter is also a result of modern farming practices. The oils used to make margarine are usually high in essential fatty acids and contain no cholesterol, but the hydrogenation process that makes these oils solid drastically reduces their quality.

Seed oils offer more nutritious possibilities than solid fats. The oils you choose should be unrefined, cold pressed and, when possible, organic. Keep them in opaque containers to protect them from light and use quickly or refrigerate. Flax oil is considered by some to be one of the best oils, as it contains large amounts of cleansing fatty acids and linolenic acid which helps break down cholesterol deposits. Soy oil is also very good if you can find an unrefined brand. Sesame, safflower and sunflower oils are excellent and readily available in natural food stores. These oils are best used fresh in salads and dressings. Corn oil is another good choice. Olive oil does not contain as many essential fatty acids as other seed oils. Try not to use cottonseed oil, which some commercial "vegetable" oils are made from, because of pesticides and other toxic substances and be careful of peanut oil which can contain a carcinogenic fungus.

Here's an important tip for stir-frying. Sauté garlic and onions first; they contain bioflavinoids which help stop rancidity of the oil which can occur when the oil is heated to a high temperature.

Nuts and Seeds

Eating whole nuts and seeds will not only provide you with high quality oil, but protein, vitamins, minerals and fiber as well. Pumpkin seeds, peanuts and sunflower seeds are among the highest of the nuts and seeds in protein.

Peanut butter isn't the only form of nut butter available. Tahini is sesame seed butter, and almond, cashew and sunflower seed butters are a delicious change of pace. Nuts and seeds can be roasted in a dry skillet or a slow oven to bring out their natural flavor without using salt or oil. Be sparing with your use of these natural foods because of the high percentage of calories they contain in the form of fats.

Organic Foods

The importance of using organically grown ingredients in a vegetarian diet can be demonstrated in two ways. Consuming animal products greatly increases your exposure to pesticides unless you're eating only organically certified meat, eggs, cheese and milk. When an animal grazes on feed or pasturage that has been treated with pesticides, these chemicals become concentrated in the fat in the muscle tissue and mammary glands of these animals. If you eat meat or the milk products from these animals, those concentrated pesticides become even more concentrated in your own fatty tissues, where they are apt to remain for a long time. They can even be passed on in human breast milk. Some studies suggest that animal products are the source of over 95% of all chemical residues now found in our food. High levels of antibiotics and growth hormones are used in meat production, both having hazardous effects on human health.

Even if you are a total vegetarian and consume no animal products of any kind, you're not immune from the effects of pesticides. Several years ago a million watermelons were removed from the marketplace in California and destroyed because over 1,000 people had become sick from the pesticide aldicarb the melons had been sprayed with. Recent information released from the National Academy of Sciences states that as many as 20,000 cancers a year could be attributed to 15 different pesticides used in common foods. The products posing the worst risk were tomatoes, oranges and wheat, with other fruits and vegetables cited, like potatoes, lettuce, apples, peaches, soybeans, beans, carrots, corn and grapes, as well as meat. Fortunately this cancer risk is much lower than that from smoking cigarettes, but unlike a smoking habit, as consumers we get no choice in the matter unless we insist on purchasing only organically grown products.

Natural food stores are an oasis for the shopper who is concerned about quality organic produce and food stuffs. Organic food accounts for almost 20% of the total sales in these stores. Perhaps one of the most important foods to consider buying organically is oil. Since the pesticides you consume become more concentrated in your fatty tissues it's important that the fats you eat are as clean as possible. Next, you might concentrate on fresh produce, as these have the best chance of coming in direct contact with pesticide sprays. Besides a natural food store, check out any local food co-ops. These are often operated by shoppers who are concerned with the quality of the food they purchase and shop for the best prices available. You should also consider buying produce from sources as close to you as possible. This way you have a better chance of finding out how your produce is grown. If these options are not available to you, Walnut Acres provides a mail order service for organic and other natural foods (Penn's Creek, PA 17862).

Macrobiotics

Macrobiotics is heavily emphasized in this book and is the basis for many of the recipes and their ingredients. Macrobiotics has played a major role in my life and is the diet I settled upon 12 years ago as the most balanced and suitable for me.

"Macro" - "Biotics" means *Great Life*. More than a diet, it means taking the necessary steps to achieve the greatest potential for health and happiness in one's life. In macrobiotics, the kitchen is seen as the center of our evolution toward health and happiness. At its foundation is a natural whole foods diet that takes into account that no two people are identical and therefore their dietary needs will be different. The diet is adapted for each person's unique condition (their state of health), their constitution (what one is born with and inherits), age, sex, type of occupation, level of activity and their mental, physical and emotional condition. Foods are selected and eaten in harmony with the natural order of life. They are chosen according to the climate one lives in, the daily weather conditions, the season, and whether the food is locally and organically grown. The importance of food in creating our blood is emphasized, and the fact that the condition of our blood determines the condition of our health. In other words, healthy soil makes healthy food, healthy food makes healthy blood and healthy blood makes a healthy person. That is why the quality of food selected is so important and so is the way it is prepared. There are "Seven Conditions of Health" macrobiotics uses to help one determine their state of health: 1. no fatigue, 2. good appetite, 3. deep and good sleep, 4. a good memory, 5. good sense of humor, 6. smartness in thinking - do you make wise decisions in life?, 7. honesty - with others and yourself.

The diet is centered around whole grains and supplemented with vegetables, soups, beans, sea vegetables, and supplementary foods such as fruit, fermented foods, seed and fish. The diet avoids highly refined processed foods, such as refined flours and grains, meat, dairy products (including milk, cheese, butter, yogurt), eggs, refined sweeteners, soda, coffee and tropical and semi-tropical fruits. I've used recipes here which include tomatoes, honey, spinach and bananas in order to keep the book more general.

This way of eating is now strongly supported by the American Heart Association, the National Cancer Institute, the National Academy of Sciences, the American Diabetic Association and others.

Macrobiotic recipes in this book are indicated by:

More Natural Foods Ingredients

Arrowroot or kuzu - Natural thickeners, good for making sauces and gravy. Mix with a little cold water first before adding to the sauce or gravy stock. After adding, stir constantly, bring to a boil and then lower the heat.

Baking Powder - I prefer kinds that do not contain any aluminum salts. Some commercial brands are aluminum-free or you can make your own. For the equivalent of 1 teaspoon of baking powder in a recipe, use ⅝ teaspoon of cream of tarter and ¼ teaspoon of baking soda. To make sodium-free baking powder, mix ¼ cup cream of tarter, ¼ cup arrowroot and 2 tablespoons of potassium bicarbonate (available in pharmacies). Store in an air-tight container, use in the same amounts as baking powder in any recipe.

Baking Soda - A teaspoon of baking soda contains 160 mg. of sodium. A teaspoon of baking powder made with cream of tarter contains 200 mg. of sodium. Potassium bicarbonate can be obtained from pharmacies and can be substituted for baking soda, and used to make sodium free baking powder. It may have a slightly bitter taste unless the recipe contains sweetener or spices.

Carob - Made from the pods or fruit of the carob tree. Unlike chocolate, it contains no theobromine (a caffein-like substance) or oxalic acid. Available in powdered form or as carob chips. Chips can be obtained that are sugar and dairy free.

Egg replacer - A powdered substitute for eggs that contains no eggs and no preservatives or flavorings. It provides structure in baked goods instead of using eggs. It can also be whipped and substituted for egg whites.

Gingerroot - The pungent, knobby root of the tropical plant *Zingebar*. A basic spice in all oriental cooking, the fresh root can be minced or grated. Wrapped tightly in plastic and kept in the refrigerator, one piece of root will last for weeks. Or it will keep indefinately in the freezer and bits shaved off as needed.

Gomasio - This is a popular macrobiotic condiment made from roasted sesame seeds and sea salt that is sprinkled on food at mealtime. You can buy it ready made at a natural foods store or make it at home (see recipe, pg. 127). Gomasio not only adds a nutty flavor to foods, but has the nutritional advantages of the sesame seeds it contains.

Mirin - This popular Japanese rice cooking wine is made from rice "koji", a bacterial mold loaded with enzymes, cooked white rice and water. Some varieties may have sugar or corn syrup added - look for the naturally brewed varieties instead. The alcohol content evaporates quickly during cooking. Mirin has a sweet flavor and can be added to dressings, marinades, sauces, dips, soups and stir frys. Try substituting it in a recipe that calls for white cooking wine.

Sea salt - Salt evaporated from sea water is rich in the trace minerals that common table salt lacks.

Sea vegetable powders - Sea vegetables such as nori, wakame and dulse can be dried and crushed to produce condiments that are rich in iron, calcium, vitamins and minerals.

Shiitake mushrooms - Large, dark Japanese mushrooms with a pungent, smoky flavor. If dried, store in an airtight container and soak in hot water for 15 minutes or longer before using.

Soba - Thin Japanese noodles made of buckwheat.

Soy sauce - There are actually two versions of soy sauce used in Japan, *shoyu* and *tamari*. They differ in the type of starter or "koji" used to produce them. Shoyu is made from soybeans, cracked wheat and sea salt, whereas tamari is made without the wheat. Shoyu should only be added to foods during the last few minutes of cooking, as the evaporation of its alcohol destroys its rich flavor and aroma. Both varieties contain glutamic acid, a natural form of monosodium glutamate (MSG), a flavor enhancer.

Spirulina - A powder made from cultivated pond-grown blue-green algae; is 60% protein and a valuable source of vitamin A (23,300 I.U. in 1 Tbsp.), B12 (330% of recommended daily allowance in 1 Tbsp.) and iron.

Suribachi - A small Japanese pottery bowl with serrated interior, used to grind sesame or other seeds.

Toasted sesame oil - This dark, delicious, nutty-flavored oil is good for stir-frying, sauces, marinades and dressing.

Udon - Thick Japanese noodles made from wheat flour.

Umeboshi plums - This is a variety of apricot pickled in red shiso leaves. It's considered a great antacid due to its high alkaline content and is high in vitamin C. They have a salty, tangy flavor that's delicious on sushi, dressings, sauces and marinades. *Umeboshi vinegar* is the juice left over after the pickling of the umeboshi plum. Use sparingly, as it very strong and tart.

Wasabi - This is the Japanese "horseradish" familiar to sushi eaters. Wasabi powder can be mixed with water to form a greenish-grey paste. It is very hot so use sparingly. Wasabi is rich in digestive enzymes. You can mix it with shoyu as a dipping sauce, spread on rice or add to broth.

Wheat berries - Unground kernels of wheat, excellent for sprouting or cooked whole like other grains.

Whole wheat pastry flour - Made from the whole grain of soft wheat, is low in gluten, makes light pastry dough and baked goods. Contains all the vitamins and minerals of whole wheat flour, which is usually made from hard winter wheat.

Natural Foods Substitutions

¼ tsp. dried, finely powdered herb = ¾ to 1 tsp. dried, loosely crumbled =
    1½ to 2 tsp. fresh chopped herb
1 Tbsp. dried onion flakes = 1 medium raw onion
½ tsp. garlic powder = 1 clove fresh garlic
1 tsp. dried dill seed = 1 stalk fresh dill
1 cup butter = 7/8 cup oil + 3 Tbsp. liquid
1 tsp. baking powder = ¼ tsp. baking soda + ½ tsp. cream of tartar
1 cup buttermilk = 1½ Tbsp. lemon juice or vinegar added to 1 cup milk
1 cup shortening = ⅔ cup oil
1 Tbsp. flour for thickening = ½ Tbsp. cornstarch
1 large lemon = ¼ cup juice
rind of one whole lemon = 1 Tbsp. grated
1 whole orange = about ½ cup juice
1 cup carob = 1½ cups cocoa
¾ Tbsp. carob = 1 square chocolate
2 tsp. dry yeast = 1 oz. compressed fresh yeast
1 Tbsp. miso = ½ tsp. salt
2 Tbsp. tamari = 1 Tbsp. miso
1 cup white flour = 1 cup whole wheat pastry flour
    or 1 cup whole wheat flour minus 2 Tbsp.

¾ cup sugar =

½ cup honey	½ cup fruit concentrate
¼ cup molasses	1½ cup rice syrup
1½ cups barley malt	2 cups apple juice
½ cup maple syrup	1 cup apple butter

When replacing sugar with a concentrated sweetener, reduce liquid in the
recipe by ¼ cup. If recipe uses no liquid, then for each ¾ cup concentrated
sweetener used add 4 Tbsp. flour.

To jell 2 cups of liquid -
2 tsp. agar powder = 4 tsp. gelatin
3 Tbsp. agar flakes = 4 tsp. gelatin
1 Tbsp. kanten flakes = 1 Tbsp. gelatin

As a thickening agent, kuzu can be used in the following proportions:
1 tsp. kuzu powder = 1 Tbsp. flour
1½ tsp. kuzu powder = 1 Tbsp. arrowroot
4½ tsp. kuzu powder = 1 Tbsp. cornstarch
1 cup thick sauce = use 1½ to 2¼ Tbsp. kuzu
1 cup jelled liquid = use 2 Tbsp. kuzu
(Always dissolve crushed kuzu first in a small amount of cold water. If using
acidic liquids, such as lemon juice, add slightly more kuzu.)

ALLURING APPETIZERS

● *Indicates macrobiotic recipe*

SUNFLOWER DIP ☯

in Sourdough Loaf

Yield: 6 cups

Great for parties and special occasions served in a bread bowl, made by scooping the insides out of a large round loaf of sourdough bread.
See photo opposite pg. 48.

Heat a dry skillet and roast over medium heat, stirring constantly until golden brown and fragrant:

1 cup of sunflower seeds

Place in food processor or blender and blend until fairly fine. Add and process until smooth:

½ cup water   **3 Tbsp. chopped scallions**
¼ cup lemon juice   **3 Tbsp. dark barley miso**
2 cloves garlic, minced   **2 Tbsp. light miso**
¼ cup chopped red onion   **2 Tbsp. tahini**

Crumble into a bowl:

2 lbs. soft tofu

Mix with the blender contents. Process until smooth, or blend in two batches then combine batches. Cut top off round loaf of sourdough bread and pull out bread inside, leaving a shell. (Bread can be used for bread pudding or crumbs). Fill with tofu mixture just before serving. Garnish with strips of red or green pepper and serve with raw vegetables.

Per ¼ cup serving: Calories: 80, Protein: 6 gm., Carbohydrates: 4 gm., Fat: 4 gm.

AVOCADO DIP

Yield: 1½ cups

Peel and mash:

1 large ripe avocado

Mix with:

¼ cup salsa sauce   **1 Tbsp. lemon or lime juice**
2 Tbsp. green onions,   **½ tsp. sea salt (optional)**
chopped

Serve with blue corn chips.

Per ¼ cup serving: Calories: 59, Protein: 3 gm., Carbohydrates: 1 gm., Fat: 2 gm.

GREEN TOFU DIP

Yield: 1½ cups

Combine in a processor or blender:

½ lb. tofu, crumbled
½ cup parsley, minced
2 Tbsp. safflower oil
2 Tbsp. lemon juice

2 green onions, chopped
2 tsp. dill weed
1 Tbsp. capers (opt.)
½ tsp. sea salt

Serve with sticks of raw vegies like cucumber, carrot, celery, green or red pepper, and zucchini.

Per ¼ cup serving: Calories: 69, Protein: 3 gm., Carbohydrates: 1 gm., Fat: 6 gm.

CASHEW CHEESE DIP

Yield: 1½ cups

Blend until smooth:

1 cup cashews
1 cup water
¼ cup onion, minced
2 Tbsp. sesame seeds

½ tsp. paprika
1 clove of garlic, minced
juice of 1 lemon

Add a little at a time, blending:

¼ cup safflower oil

Serve with crackers.

Per 2 Tbsp. serving: Calories: 117, Protein: 3 gm., Carbohydrates: 4 gm., Fat: 5 gm.

PIMENTO SPREAD

Yield: 2 cups

Combine in a food processor or blender:

1 lb. tofu
¼ cup oil
¼ cup lemon juice

2 Tbsp. chopped red onion
¾ tsp. sea salt

Mix until smooth, using a rubber scraper to push down sides.

Add and blend in:

1-4 oz. jar pimentos, chopped

Pour into serving bowl and chill.

Per serving: Calories: 108, Protein: 5 gm., Carbohydrates: 3 gm., Fat: 9 gm.

HOLIDAY NUT BALL ☯

Yield: about 3 cups

Steam for 20 minutes, set aside to cool, then grate:
½ lb. tempeh, defrosted

Roast in a dry skillet until lightly browned:
2 cups whole almonds, unblanched

Finely chop the almonds with a knife or in a food processor and set aside.

Mix the grated tempeh by hand or in a processor with:

¾ cup Tofu Mayonnaise   **3 Tbsp. nutritional yeast**
(pg. 75)   **2 Tbsp. tamari**

If mixture seems dry, add a spoonful of water. Stir in half the finely chopped almonds. Chill mixture several hours until firm. Shape into a ball and roll in remaining chopped almonds. Place on a plate and surround with crackers.

Per serving: Calories: 226, Protein: 10 gm., Carbohydrates: 8 gm., Fat: 10 gm.

MANDARIN TEMPEH RIBLETS

Yield: 6-8 servings

Steam for 10 minutes;
½ lb. tempeh, defrosted

Cool, cut cake in half crosswise, then in 1 inch strips.

Make a marinade with:

¼ cup tamari   **2 Tbsp. minced fresh ginger**
2 Tbsp. oil   **½ tsp. garlic powder**
2 Tbsp. honey (or ¼ cup   **½ tsp. Chinese 5-Spice**
brown rice syrup)   **powder***
2 Tbsp. water

Marinate all day or overnight. Spread in a single layer in a baking dish and bake uncovered at 350° for 20 minutes, basting with marinade half way through. Riblets can be served as "finger food" or cut in half and placed on toothpicks.

*Available in Oriental food shops, or substitute 1 tsp. allspice mixed with ¼ tsp. cayenne pepper.

Per serving: Calories: 126, Protein: 7 gm., Carbohydrates: 8 gm., Fat: 7 gm.

LENTIL WALNUT PATE

Yield: makes 3½ cups

Cut into small cubes:
> **8 slices rye bread**

Pour over bread (should be 2 cups, packed):
> **1 cup hot vegetable stock**

Let bread soak while cooking lentils. Combine in pan:
> **2½ cups water**   **3 cloves garlic, cut up**
> **1 cup brown lentils, washed**   **1 bay leaf**
>   **½ tsp. kelp**

Bring lentils to a boil, reduce heat, cover and cook 35-40 minutes until tender. Liquid should be absorbed, but lentils moist. Remove bay leaf.

While lentils cook, saute in a hot skillet:
> **1 onion, chopped fine**
> **2 tsp. dark sesame oil**
> **2 tsp. fresh ginger, minced**

When onions are soft, sprinkle with:
> **1 Tbsp. tamari**   **1 tsp. thyme**
> **1 Tbsp. mirin**   **pinch of cayenne**
> **1 tsp. marjoram**

Crumb in blender:
> **¼ cup walnuts**

Put walnuts with bread. Mix onions with the lentils and puree in blender or processor. Mix well with the soaked bread cubes. Heat oven to 350⁰. Taste pate and add a little sea salt if desired. Pack into a well-oiled round quart pan. Cover with foil. Place pan in a larger pan of hot water. Bake 45 minutes, remove foil, bake 15 more. Cool 30 minutes, run a knife around sides of pan to loosen and invert loaf on serving plate.

Top with:
> **¼ cup walnuts, chopped fine**

Surround pate with crackers or melba toast.

Per ¼ cup serving: Calories: 102, Protein: 5 gm., Carbohydrates: 14 gm., Fat: 3 gm.

Variation: Use toasted sesame seeds instead of walnuts.

HUMMUS

Yield: 4 cups

Delicious stuffed in pita bread for a sandwich or as a spread on crackers.

Rinse and soak overnight:
> **1½ cups raw chickpeas**

Drain, add:
> **4 cups water**
> **¼ tsp. kelp**

Bring to a boil. Reduce heat, cover, cook until tender, 50-60 minutes.

Cool beans, drain, mash or process to a thick paste, adding:

> **¼ cup tahini**   **juice of 1 large or 2 small**
> **⅓ cup fresh minced parsley**   **lemons**
> **¼ cup green onions, minced**   **3 cloves garlic, minced**
> **2 Tbsp. light miso**   **1/8 tsp. cayenne**

Chill overnight or a few hours so flavors mellow.

Per ½ cup serving: Calories: 161, Protein: 7 gm., Carbohydrates: 18 gm., Fat: 11 gm.

MISO TAHINI SPREAD

Yield: about ½ cup

Mix well together:

> **¼ cup tahini**   **3 Tbsp. miso**
> **¼ cup water**   **½ tsp. marjoram**
> **2 Tbsp. grated onion**

Good spread on Brown Rice Sesame Bread (pg. 43)

Per 1 Tbsp. serving: Calories: 69, Protein: 2 gm., Carbohydrates: 4 gm., Fat: 10 gm.

Variation: Instead of grated raw onion, add 2 cups diced green onions that have been sautéed in 2 tsp. sesame oil.

BRIGHT BREAKFASTS

● *Indicates macrobiotic recipe*

JUDY'S RISE AND SHINE MUESLI

Yield: 4 servings

Mix all ingredients together and soak overnight in a sealed thermos or a covered container kept in refrigerator:

2¼ cups water (or use 1¼ cups water and 1 cup soy-milk or apple juice)
1½ cups oat flakes
¼ cup sunflower seeds

¼ cup raisins
¼ cup chopped nuts
1 tsp. cinnamon
1 apple or pear, grated

This recipe is based on the popular cereal created by Swiss doctor, Max Bircher-Benner. He made it famous as part of his healing system based on a diet high in raw foods. Soaking the grains overnight breaks down the starches into natural sugars, making them not only sweet, but easy to digest. For young children, all the ingredients can be combined in a blender or processor just before serving, making a nourishing puree.

Per serving: Calories: 352, Protein: 12 gm., Carbohydrates: 52 gm., Fat: 8 gm.

Fruit Muesli: Add a handful of strawberries, raspberries or pitted sweet cherries to the cereal just before serving.

Banana Topping for Muesli: Mash a banana with a little soy yogurt.

Dried Fruit Muesli: Substitute dried apricots, dates, figs or other fruit for the apple. Snip small with scissors.

CREAMY BROWN RICE CEREAL

Yield: 4 servings

Wash several times until water is clear:
1 cup short grain brown rice

Combine in 2-quart pan with:
5 cups water
a pinch of sea salt

Bring to a boil, then cover, reduce heat to simmer and cook about 50 minutes until creamy consistency. Top each bowl with toasted sesame or sunflower seeds.

Per serving: Calories: 134, Protein: 3 gm., Carbohydrates: 29 gm., Fat: 0 gm.

RICE BARLEY CREAM CEREAL

Yield: 6 servings

Wash, drain and soak overnight:
1 cup barley

Wash well:
2 cups brown rice

Combine grains with:
5 cups water
pinch of sea salt

Bring to a boil. Turn heat to low and simmer 50 minutes. It should have a creamy consistency.

Sprinkle on as a garnish:
½ to 1 cup sunflower seeds, toasted

Per serving: Calories: 396, Protein: 17 gm., Carbohydrates: 101 gm., Fat: 2 gm.

MOM'S CRUNCHY GRANOLA

Yield: 9 cups

Blanch by dropping into boiling water for 1 minute, then slip skins from:
½ cup whole almonds

Combine and heat in a small saucepan:
½ cup barley malt or brown   **¼ cup vegetable oil**
rice syrup   **1 tsp. vanilla**

Mix in a large bowl:
5 cups rolled oats   **½ cup sesame seeds**
½ cup sunflower seeds,   **½ cup flaked coconut**
toasted   **½ cup raw walnuts**
½ cup wheat germ   **½ cup peanuts (opt.)**

Stir in liquids and almonds. Spread evenly on a cookie sheet. Bake at 325° for 30 to 45 minutes until golden brown, stirring often. Cool, then store in an airtight container.

Per ½ cup serving: Calories: 293, Protein: 10 gm., Carbohydrates: 32 gm., Fat: 10 gm.

NUTTY BANANA BARLEY

Yield: 4 servings

You may substitute wheat berries (soaked overnight) for barley or rice.

Bring 2 cups water to a boil in a large pan. Add:
> **½ cup whole barley**
> **½ cup brown rice**

Bring back to a boil, lower heat, cover, simmer 45 minutes until grains are tender. Mix in:
> **5 dried figs, finely sliced**
> **1 banana, sliced**
> **¼ cup walnuts or pecans, chopped**

Serve warm for a delicious breakfast, or chill and mix with Sweet Sesame Dressing (pg. 76) for a salad.

Per serving: Calories: 226, Protein: 6 gm., Carbohydrates: 60 gm., Fat: 4 gm.

NO-EGG "OMELETS"

Yield: 4 servings (16 crepes)

Little crepes, that can be spread with fruit butter and rolled up, or filled with vegetables for a lunch dish.

Combine in a blender or beat well by hand:

> **3 cups soymilk**
> **1 Tbsp. oil**
> **2 cups whole wheat pastry flour**

> **⅓ cup nutritional yeast flakes***
> **½ tsp. baking powder**
> **½ tsp. sea salt**

Beat out any lumps. (Batter can be made ahead and will keep in the refrigerator). Heat a 9″ skillet, add a few drops of oil and tip pan to coat bottom. Pour ¼ cup batter into pan and immediately tip and rotate the ban so batter spreads out into a thin circle. Cook over medium high heat until top starts to dry out, flip over and cook other side briefly.

Per serving: Calories: 356, Protein: 15 gm., Carbohydrates: 51 gm., Fat: 10 gm.

*Use only *saccharomyces cerevisiae*, a cheesy-tasting, easily digestible nutritional yeast.

TEMPEH BREAKFAST SAUSAGE

Yield: 6 servings

Steam for 10 minutes, cool and grate on the coarse side of the grater:
½ lb. defrosted tempeh

Combine grated tempeh with:

⅓ cup water   **½ tsp. sage**
2 Tbsp. whole wheat flour **½ tsp. thyme**
1 Tbsp. oil   **¼ tsp. marjoram**
1 Tbsp. dark miso   **¼ tsp. garlic powder**
                              ¼ tsp. cayenne

Mix well and shape into 6 flat cakes, pressing together firmly. (Add a little flour if mixture is too moist). Fry in a hot skillet until browned, in just enough oil to keep patties from sticking to the pan. Drain on paper towel. Patties can be made ahead and frozen; separate each one by waxed paper.

Per serving: Calories: 113, Protein: 8 gm., Carbohydrates: 5 gm., Fat: 6 gm.

MEXICAN SCRAMBLED TOFU

Yield: 4 servings

Heat a skillet and saute:

2 Tbsp. safflower oil   1 onion, chopped
2 jalapeños or hot peppers, 1 green or red pepper, chopped
  chopped

Mash some, crumble remainder of:
1 lb. tofu

Add to skillet with:

1 tomato, chopped   **½ cup grated jalapeño or**
½ cup salsa   cheddar soy cheese (opt.)

Stir fry a few minutes. Season if desired with a pinch of basil, oregano and garlic powder. Serve alone, with corn grits or on toasted English muffins. Protect your hands with rubber gloves when working with hot peppers.

Per serving: Calories: 175, Protein: 10 gm., Carbohydrates: 9 gm., Fat: 12 gm.

FRENCH TOAST

Yield: 4 slices

Whisk together in a flat bowl:
1 cup soymilk
½ tsp. sea salt
2 Tbsp. whole wheat pastry
flour

1 Tbsp. nutritional yeast *
1 tsp. honey or barley malt

Heat a pan with a little oil. Dip into mixture, coating both sides:
4 slices whole wheat bread

Fry until golden brown. Serve hot with maple syrup.

*Use only *saccharomyces cerevisiae*, a cheesy-tasting, easily digestible nutritional yeast.

Per slice: Calories: 133, Protein: 5 gm., Carbohydrates: 18 gm., Fat: 5 gm.

MOCHI WAFFLES

Yield: 1 serving

Cut in half:
2· 1 ½ oz. plain or cinnamon-raisin mochi bars

Place a piece in each section of a preheated waffle iron. Cook like a waffle.
Serve with Mother Nature's Apple Butter (pg. 126) or Fruit Syrup (pg. 40). Eat
mochi waffles as soon as they come off the griddle; if left to cool, they will
harden.

Per serving: Calories: 150, Protein: 3 gm., Carbohydrates: 32 gm., Fat: 1 gm.

Fruit Syrup

Yield: 1 cup

Combine in a small saucepan:
1 cup apple or grape concentrate
2 Tbsp. arrowroot

Heat until thickened. Use as a topping for pancakes, waffles or French toast.

Per ¼ cup serving: Calories: 75, Protein: 0 gm., Carbohydrates: 18 gm., Fat: 0 gm.

BOUNTIFUL BREADS

SANDWICH-AS-A-MEAL

● *Indicates macrobiotic recipe*

SESAME HERB CRACKERS

Yield: 3 dozen

Mix together:

>   **2 cups whole wheat flour**
>   **½ cup sesame seeds**
>   **2 Tbsp. wheat germ**
>   **2 Tbsp. bran**
>
>   **½ tsp. each of: oregano,**
>   **basil, garlic powder, dried**
>   **parsley**

Stir in:

>   **¾ cup cold water**
>   **4 Tbsp. sesame oil**

Roll dough out onto a lightly oiled cookie sheet or roll thinly between two pieces of waxed paper and transfer to sheet. Cut into squares or diamond shapes before baking. Bake in a preheated oven at 400° for 17-20 minutes. Cool, break apart.

Per cracker: Calories: 50, Protein: 1 gm., Carbohydrates: 5 gm., Fat: 2 gm.

Variations: Substitute ¼ cup onion flakes for the bran and wheat germ. Or try adding ¼ cup grated soy jalapeño or cheddar cheese to dough. Or use sunflower seeds, lightly crushed.

RYE CRACKERS

Yield: 7 dozen small crackers

Mix together:

>   **1 cup rye flour**
>   **1 cup whole wheat flour**
>   **¼ cup caraway seeds**
>   **2 Tbsp. wheat germ**
>
>   **1 tsp. baking powder**
>   **½ tsp. sea salt**
>   **½ tsp. garlic powder**

Stir in, to make a stiff dough:

>   **3 Tbsp. sesame oil**
>   **⅔ cup soy milk**

Divide dough into 2 balls. Roll out very thin onto 2 lightly oiled cookie sheets. Make pieces 2″ x 1½″. Preheat oven to 425° and bake 7 to 10 minutes, watching to be sure they don't burn.

Per serving: Calories: 62, Protein: 2 gm., Carbohydrates: 9 gm., Fat: 3 gm.

MEXICAN CORN BREAD ☯

Yield: 9 squares

Combine:

1 cup corn meal	**½ cup whole wheat flour**
½ cup whole wheat pastry	**2 tsp. baking powder**
flour	**pinch of sea salt**

Add:

½ cup corn kernels
2 Tbsp. chopped jalapeños or hot peppers

Add and mix with a fork for several minutes. Stir in:

1 cup soy milk	**½ cup water**
½ cup grated soy jalapeno	**⅓ cup oil**
cheese (opt.)	**2 Tbsp. rice syrup or honey**

Spread into an oiled 9″ x 9″ baking dish. Bake at 425° for 25-30 minutes. Allow to sit for 15 minutes before serving. If you use soy cheese, it may make the bread appear runny when hot.

Per square: Calories: 145, Protein: 3 gm., Carbohydrates: 16 gm., Fat: 9 gm.

CORN STICKS

Yield: 14 sticks

See photo opposite pg. 49.

Heat oven to 400°. Heat corn stick pans and brush with oil before filling. Mix in a bowl:

1 cup yellow cornmeal	**2 tsp. baking powder**
1 cup whole wheat pastry	**1 tsp. sea salt**
flour	

Mix in another bowl, then stir into dry ingredients:

1 cup water or soymilk
¼ cup oil
1 tsp. honey

Pour into hot, oiled pans and bake at 400° for 20 minutes. Or make corn muffins by filling 12 oiled muffin tins with batter.

Per stick: Calories: 132, Protein: 2 gm., Carbohydrates: 13 gm., Fat: 9 gm.

BROWN RICE SESAME BREAD

Yield: 1 loaf

A hearty, dense yeast-free bread. Using grains in bread requires fermenting time which varies with the seasons. Dough will be sticky, knead with wet hands.

Combine in a bowl and mix well:

3 cups whole wheat flour
1 cup cornmeal
¼ tsp. sea salt

½ cup unhulled roasted
sesame seeds

Add and work in your hands:

1¼ cups cooked short grain brown rice

Spread the mixture out to make a well in the center, add:

1¼ cups warm water
1 tsp. miso dissolved in ¼ cup warm water

Mix with a wooden spoon, adding a little more water if needed to make a moist bread dough. Knead for about 15 minutes, until dough comes together. It will be sticky. Have ready a well-oiled bowl. Place dough in bowl and turn over twice to coat with oil. Lightly oil a sheet of waxed paper and place oiled side down on top of dough. Dampen a towel and cover bowl. Keep in a cool place for 13 to 15 hours in the summer, 24-26 hours in winter. Place dough in an oiled loaf pan. Make a cut down the center. Place pan in a cold oven. Turn heat to 200⁰ and bake for 25 minutes. Raise heat to 350⁰ and bake 1 hour. Loaf should be well browned and starting to pull away from sides of pan. Cool. Delicious served with Miso Tahini Spread (pg. 34).

Per slice: Calories: 145, Protein: 5 gm., Carbohydrates: 26 gm., Fat: 1 gm.

WHOLE WHEAT CROUTONS

Yield: 3½ cups

Mix:

1 Tbsp. sesame oil
1 Tbsp. grated soy parmesan
cheese (opt.)

¼ tsp. each basil and
oregano
dash garlic powder

Spread lightly on bread.

Cut into ¾″ cubes:

4 slices whole grain bread

Place on cookie sheet and bake at 250° for 30 minutes until crisp. Store in a tightly covered container in refrigerator.

Per ¼ cup serving: Calories: 25, Protein: 1 gm., Carbohydrates: 4 gm., Fat: 1 gm.

WHOLE WHEAT ENGLISH MUFFINS

Yield: 12 4" muffins

Place in a large bowl to foam:

¼ cup warm water
2 Tbsp. yeast

1 Tbsp. barley malt or 2 tsp.
honey

Stir in:

4 cups whole wheat flour (or
half unbleached flour)

1 cup water
2 Tbsp. safflower oil
½ tsp. sea salt

Knead dough 10 minutes on a floured work surface. Roll out and cut into a dozen 4" rounds. Dust a baking sheet with cornmeal, place muffins on sheet. Let rise for 1 hour in a warm place. Bake at 350° for about 25 minutes.

Per muffin: Calories: 158, Protein: 6 gm., Carbohydrates: 30 gm., Fat: 2 gm.

Raisin Muffins: Add ½ cup raisins and ½ tsp. cinnamon to the dough.

WHOLE WHEAT BISCUITS

Yield: 16 to 18 biscuits

Mix in a bowl with fork or fingers:

3 cups whole wheat pastry
flour
½ cup safflower oil

4 tsp. baking powder
½ tsp. sea salt

Stir in:

2/3 cup cold soymilk (or water)

Knead on a lightly floured board about 25 times. Roll or pat out ½" thick. Cut rounds with a 2" cutter and place on a lightly oiled sheet. Preheat oven to 425° and bake 15 minutes. For a fluffier biscuit, use ½ cup soy margarine instead of oil.

Per biscuit: Calories: 133, Protein: 4 gm., Carbohydrates: 16 gm., Fat: 7 gm.

BREAD STICKS

Yield: 24 sticks

Place in a bowl and let stand 5 minutes:

1 Tbsp. yeast   **¼ cup warm water**
1 tsp. barley malt

Add:

3 cups whole wheat flour   **2 Tbsp. nutritional yeast**
¾ cup warm water   **(opt.)**
¼ cup oil   **1 tsp. sea salt**

Mix dough until it forms a ball, then knead 10 minutes until smooth. Oil a bowl, turn dough around to coat, then cover dough and let rise until double. Press dough down, break off 24 pieces. Roll each into sticks about 8″ long. If desired, roll sticks in sesame or caraway seeds. Place on oiled baking sheet. Cover with waxed paper and let rise again. Bake at 400° for 5 minutes, turn over with tongs, bake 5 to 7 minutes more.

Per stick: Calories: 72, Protein: 2 gm., Carbohydrates: 11 gm., Fat: 3 gm.

Onion Twists: Chop 1 onion finely, saute in the oil before mixing with the dough. Twist each stick.

RYE ROLLS with CARAWAY

See photo between pgs. 80-81.   *Yield: 12 rolls*

Place in a bowl to "work":

2 Tbsp. barley malt or honey
1 Tbsp. yeast   **¼ cup warm water**

Add:

2 cups whole wheat flour   **¼ cup sesame or sunflower**
1½ cups rye flour   **oil**
1 cup water   **½ tsp. sea salt**

Knead 10 minutes until dough feels elastic, working in:

1 Tbsp. caraway seeds

Oil a bowl, turn dough around in it to coat, then cover bowl with a damp towel and place in a warm place to rise. Let rise 1 to 2 hours until double. Gently press down. Shape dough into 12 balls, place on a lightly oiled baking sheet. Cover with damp towel, let rise 45 minutes to 1 hour. Preheat oven to 375° and bake rolls 18 to 20 minutes.

Per roll: Calories: 161, Protein: 4 gm., Carbohydrates: 27 gm., Fat: 5 gm.

MILLET DATE MUFFINS

Yield: 12 muffins

Preheat oven to 400°. Oil or place paper liners in muffin tins.

Mix dry ingredients together:

1½ cups whole wheat pastry flour
3 tsp. baking powder

⅔ cup cooked leftover millet
½ tsp. sea salt

Mix in another bowl:

1 cup water
½ cup cut up dates
⅓ cup oil

2 Tbsp. honey or ¼ cup barley malt

Combine wet and dry ingredients but do not overmix. Spoon into muffin tins. Bake at 400° for 20 minutes.

Per muffin: Calories: 131, Protein: 2 gm., Carbohydrates: 18 gm., Fat: 6 gm.

HEALTHY BURGER BUNS

Yield: 8 large buns

In a large bowl, combine and let foam:

¼ cup warm water
1 Tbsp. yeast

1 tsp. barley malt syrup or honey

Stir in, using your hands as dough gets stiff:

3 to 3 ½ cups whole wheat flour
1 cup water

2 Tbsp. toasted sesame seeds (opt.)
½ tsp. sea salt

Knead for about 10 minutes on lightly floured surface. Oil a clean bowl, turn dough around to coat, cover bowl with a warm, damp towel and let rise until double in a warm draft-free place.

Toast in a 350° oven in a flat pan for 10 minutes:

2 Tbsp. toasted sesame seeds (opt.)

Press dough down, divide into 8 balls. Flatten into ½″ thick rounds, pressing top of dough into the seeds. Place seed side up on a lightly oiled baking sheet. Lay a piece of waxed paper loosely over the top of the rolls, let them rise double. Heat oven to 375° and bake buns 16 to 18 minutes. Remove to rack to cool.

Per bun: Calories: 184, Protein: 6 gm., Carbohydrates: 33 gm., Fat: 4 gm.

HERBED YEAST ROLLS

Yield: 24 rolls

See photo opposite pg. 49.

Let stand for 5 minutes:

1 Tbsp. yeast
½ cup warm water

¼ cup barley malt (or 2 Tbsp. honey)

Stir in:

3 cups whole wheat flour
3 cups unbleached white flour
1½ cups water
½ cup safflower oil

1 tsp. oregano
½ tsp. sea salt
½ tsp. thyme
½ tsp. dill

Mix until a ball of dough forms. Knead dough on lightly floured surface until elastic. Oil a bowl lightly, turn dough around to coat, cover with a damp towel and let rise in a warm place until double. Knead down and pull apart to form small balls. Grease 2 dozen muffin tins. Place 3 small balls in each section to make cloverleafs. Let rise 1 hour. Bake at 375° for about 20 minutes. Remove from tins and serve while hot.

Per roll: Calories: 147, Protein: 4 gm., Carbohydrates: 23 gm., Fat: 5 gm.

BLUEBERRY COFFEE CAKE

Yield: 9 squares

Mix in a bowl:

2½ cups whole wheat pastry flour

2 tsp. baking powder
½ tsp. sea salt

Have ready:

2 cups fresh or frozen blueberries

Mix in another bowl:

1 cup soymilk or water
⅓ cup honey
¼ cup oil

1 tsp. egg replacer in 1 Tbsp. water

Stir dry ingredients into liquids, adding berries last. Pour into an oiled 9″ x 9″ pan. Bake at 375° for 35-40 minutes, until top springs back when lightly pressed.

Per square: Calories: 209, Protein: 5 gm., Carbohydrates: 34 gm., Fat: 7 gm.

Sunflower Dip in Sourdough Loaf, pg. 30

HOLIDAY FRUIT BRAID

Yield: 1 large loaf (20 slices)

A beautiful and delicious bread that can be made ahead, as the fruit keeps it from drying out. See photo opposite pg. 49.

Bring to a boil in a small saucepan:

1 cup dried papaya, snipped small with a scissors

½ cup dried apricots, snipped small

1 cup water

Cover, remove from heat and let stand 15 minutes.

Combine in a large bowl:

1 Tbsp. yeast

¼ cup warm water

¼ cup safflower oil

¼ cup honey

Mix and add:

2 tsp. egg replacer in 2 Tbsp. water

¼ tsp. nutmeg

2 tsp. finely shredded lemon peel

¼ tsp. mace

Drain liquid from the dried fruit into a measuring cup and add enough water to make 1 cup liquid. Add to yeast and seasonings.

Stir in:

3 ½ cups whole wheat pastry flour

½ cup pecans, coarsely chopped

Add more flour as needed to make a firm dough, working in the dried fruit, kneading bread about 10 minutes. Oil a bowl and turn dough around in it to coat. Cover with a damp towel and put in a warm place until double in bulk (1 to 1 ½ hours). Press dough down, divide into 4 balls. Lightly oil a baking sheet. Roll and stretch 3 of the balls into long ropes and braid these on the sheet. Divide remaining ball into 3 pieces and make the 3 smaller ropes into a braid, laying this on top of large braid. Let rise 45 minutes to 1 hour. Preheat oven to 350° and bake 35 to 40 minutes. Remove from pan and cool. Decorate if desired: press pieces of dried fruit (such as dried pineapple or papaya) on top in any pattern you like, use a dab of honey to make them stick.

Per slice: Calories: 130, Protein: 4 gm., Carbohydrates: 26 gm., Fat: 1 gm.

Herbed Yeast Rolls, pg. 48
Corn Sticks, pg. 43
Holiday Fruit Bread, pg. 49

SANDWICH-AS-A-MEAL

AVOCADO RUEBENS

Yield: 4 sandwiches

Mash together:
>   2 ripe avocadoes   ¼ cup chopped green onions
>   1 small tomato, chopped   2 Tbsp. salsa sauce
>   1 clove garlic, minced

Spread on:
>   4 slices whole grain bread

Top with:
>   1 cup drained sauerkraut   grated soy cheese (opt.)
>   ¼ cup Thousand Island Dressing (pg. 75)

Top with:
>   4 slices bread

Lightly oil a large skillet, turn heat to medium. Place 2 sandwiches in the pan and grill. If using soy cheese, place a lid on to help cheese melt. Turn sandwich when brown on the bottom. Watch that they don't burn.

Per sandwich: Calories: 352, Protein: 8 gm., Carbohydrates: 36 gm., Fat: 9 gm.

TEMPEH PIZZA BURGERS

Yield: 6 servings

Have ready
>   6 Whole Wheat English Muffins (pg. 45), split
>   ½ lb. tempeh, steamed 10 minutes

Heat a large skillet, and saute:
>   2 Tbsp. olive oil
>   1 medium onion, chopped   1 green pepper, chopped

Grate tempeh on the coarse side of grater and add to onions.

Stir in and cook 5 minutes:
>   2 Tbsp. tamari   ½ tsp. marjoram
>   1 tsp. oregano   ¼ tsp. red pepper flakes
>   1 tsp. basil

Stir in:
> **1-8 oz. can tomato puree**

Place muffin halves on a cookie sheet and place under broiler to toast lightly. Set oven temperature to 375°. Spread muffins evenly with tempeh mixture. Grated soy cheese can be placed on top. Heat in oven for 10 minutes, cheese should be melted.

Per serving: Calories: 313, Protein: 15 gm., Carbohydrates: 35 gm., Fat: 10 gm.

SLOPPY RON'S

Yield: 4 servings

Lunch can be ready in 10 minutes with these!

Defrost and press out excess liquid from:
> **1 lb. frozen tofu**

Slice or pull tofu into thin strips and pieces.

Add tofu to:
> **1 cup Quick Barbecue Sauce (pg. 128)**

Heat and pile into warm buns.

Per serving: Calories: 496, Protein: 15 gm., Carbohydrates: 75 gm., Fat: 19 gm.

LINDSEY'S FAVORITE TACOS

Yield: 10 tacos

An easy to fix lunch for little ones at home.

Have ready:

> **2 cups cooked brown rice**
> **2 cups chopped Bibb or Boston lettuce**
> **10 taco shells (yellow or blue corn)**
>
> **1 small can black olives, chopped**
> **1 chopped tomato**
> **1 cucumber, thinly sliced**

Sprinkle rice with a dash of tamari, mix with chopped olives. Warm shells, fill with a few slices of cucumber, some rice, lettuce, tomato and top with taco sauce.

Per taco: Calories: 130, Protein: 3 gm., Carbohydrates: 23 gm., Fat: 4 gm.

QUICK & EASY MINI-PIZZA

Yield: 1 serving

Split in half:
> **1 whole wheat English muffin**

Spread it to the edges with:
> **2 Tbsp. tomato sauce**

Cover each half with:
> **2 slices non-dairy mozzarella**   **2 olives, chopped**
> **cheese**   **1 Tbsp. chopped onion**
> **2 mushrooms, sliced**

Sprinkle on top:
> **1/8 tsp. each oregano, basil**

Place under broiler unit and broil until cheese is bubbly.

Per pizza: Calories: 366, Protein: 13 gm., Carbohydrates: 33 gm., Fat: 16 gm.

TOSTADAS

Yield: 12

Crumble into a bowl:
> **1 lb. tofu**

Mix seasonings, then mix into the tofu:
> **1 Tbsp. whole wheat flour**   **1 tsp. barley malt powder**
> **1 Tbsp. chili powder**   **(opt.)**
> **1 tsp. garlic powder**   **½ tsp. sea salt**
> **1 tsp. cumin**

Heat in a skillet:
> **2 Tbsp. corn oil**

Cook seasoned tofu a few minutes, until warmed through. Keep warm.

Fry and drain on paper towels:
> **12 corn tortillas**

Put tortillas on platter, spoon on tofu mixture and toppings of choice: onion rings, shredded lettuce, chopped tomatoes, sliced mushrooms, salsa, or non-dairy grated cheese.

Per tostada: Calories: 112, Protein: 5 gm., Carbohydrates: 15 gm., Fat: 5 gm.

SCRUMPTIOUS SOUPS

Black Bean Soup ●   60
Cabbage Patch Soup   58
Calico Bean Soup ●   59
Chilled Basil Tomato Soup   54
Creamy Corn Chowder ●   55
French Onion Soup ●   57
Hearty Vegetable Soup ●   54
Leek Shiitake Soup ●   56
Lemon Barley Soup ●   56
Lentil Vegetable Soup ●   58
Miso Wakame Soup ●   60
Split Pea Soup ●   55

● *Indicates macrobiotic recipe*

CHILLED BASIL TOMATO SOUP

Yield: 8 servings

Puree in a blender or processor:

2-35 oz. cans plum tomatoes,
    drained
4 Tbsp. fresh basil, minced
2 Tbsp. safflower oil

2 Tbsp. brown rice vinegar
2 Tbsp. brown rice syrup
1 tsp. tamari

Chill for 2 hours, if possible. Toast in a dry skillet:
½ cup chopped walnuts

Serve soup topped with walnuts and garnish with a sprig of fresh basil.

Per serving: Calories: 144, Protein: 4 gm., Carbohydrates: 15 gm., Fat: 8 gm.

Variation: For a real treat, substitute balsamic vinegar for the brown rice vinegar.

HEARTY VEGETABLE SOUP

Yield: 6 servings

Rinse and drain:
1 cup brown rice

Add to a large kettle with:

6 cups water
1 rutabaga, diced
1 sweet potato, chopped
1 white turnip, diced

1 medium onion, cut in
    chunks
2 carrots, cut chunky

Bring to a boil, lower heat, cover and cook on medium low heat for 45 minutes. Add 1 to 2 cups water if too thick. Add:
2 cups chopped kale, well rinsed

Cook 15 minutes, then dissolve together and stir in:
¼ cup light miso
½ cup water

Do not boil after adding miso, or its friendly enzymes will be destroyed.

Per serving: Calories: 191, Protein: 6 gm., Carbohydrates: 41 gm., Fat: ⅓ gm.

CREAMY CORN CHOWDER ☯

Yield: 6 servings

Oat flakes add protein and creaminess to this tasty soup.

Saute together for 5 minutes in a big soup pot:

1 Tbsp. sesame oil   **2 tsp. fresh ginger, minced**
1 cup onions, minced   **2 stalks celery, chopped**

Add, and bring to a boil:

6 cups water   **kernels of 6 corn cobs**

Reduce heat, cover and simmer 20 minutes.

While vegies cook, soak:

½ cup rolled oats   **½ cup water**

Add to soup with:

2 Tbsp. tahini   **1 baked potato, chopped**
1 Tbsp. tamari

Simmer 20-25 minutes, Garnish with sprigs of fresh parsley and serve with Sesame Herb Crackers (pg. 42).

Per serving: Calories: 233, Protein: 8 gm., Carbohydrates: 38 gm., Fat: 10 gm.

SPLIT PEA SOUP ☯

Yield: 6 servings

Rinse split peas, then combine with water and vegetables.

2 cups green split peas   **1 onion, chopped**
6 cups water   **2 carrots, chopped chunky**

Cook 45 minutes until peas are tender. Stir in:

1 tsp. ginger powder   **1 tsp. thyme**

Dissolve together:

2 Tbsp. light miso   **¼ cup warm water**

Stir into soup. Simmer a few minutes but do not boil after adding miso.

Per serving: Calories: 198, Protein: 13 gm., Carbohydrates: 38 gm., Fat: 1 gm.

LEEK SHIITAKE SOUP

Yield: 6 servings

See photo opposite pg. 80.

Pour a cup of boiling water over:
> **5 shiitake mushrooms**

Let soak 20 minutes, remove mushrooms and chop.

Chop bottom ends off:
> **2 large leeks**

Wash ends, boil 10 minutes for stock with:
> **6 cups water**   **1 7" piece wakame**

Remove and discard ends, remove and chop wakame. Clean rest of leeks carefully, slice white and green parts, keeping separate.

Heat a pan, and fry briefly:
> **1 Tbsp. sesame oil**
> **the sliced white part of leeks**   **the chopped green leek tops**

Sauté 3 minutes, then add and sauté each for 1 minute:
> **1 celery stalk with leaves,**   **2 scallions, chopped**
> **chopped**   **(optional)**
> **2 small carrots, sliced, cut in** **the chopped shiitake**
> **half**   **mushrooms**

Add to kettle with:
> **chopped wakame**   **1 Tbsp. tamari**

Simmer for 10 minutes. Taste and add a little more tamari if desired. Top each bowl with Whole Wheat Croutons (pg. 44) and minced parsley.

Per serving: Calories: 35, Protein: 1 gm., Carbohydrates: 3 gm., Fat: 2 gm.

LEMON BARLEY SOUP

Yield: 6 servings

Sauté until lightly toasted:
> **1 Tbsp. sesame oil**
> **½ cup barley (hato mugi opt., see pg. 9)**

Place in a soup pot with:
>**5 cups soup stock**

Bring to a boil and cook, covered, 30 minutes.

Heat pan and sauté:
>**1 Tbsp. sesame oil**   **2 onions, chopped**
>**3 carrots, sliced in half**   **3 stalks celery, chopped**
>**moons**

Add to soup pot and simmer 10 minutes.

Stir in:
>**1 cup chopped kale**   **2 Tbsp. tamari**
>**⅓ cup lemon juice**   **2 tsp. dill weed**

Simmer soup 10 minutes.

Just before serving, sprinkle with:
>**3 Tbsp. minced parsley**

Per serving: Calories: 150, Protein: 4 gm., Carbohydrates: 24 gm., Fat: 5 gm.

FRENCH ONION SOUP
with Miso

Yield: 4-6 servings

Heat in a heavy pan:
>**2 Tbsp. sesame oil (plain or dark)**

Add and cook slowly for 1 hour, stirring often:
>**8 medium onions, thinly sliced**

Add:
>**3 cups vegetable stock or warm water**

Bring to a boil and simmer 5 minutes. Dissolve:
>**2 Tbsp. dark barley or brown rice miso**
>**2 Tbsp. light miso**
>**½ cup warm water or stock**

Stir miso mixture into soup, cook 5 minutes more. Serve with Whole Wheat Croutons (pg. 44) and soy parmesan cheese.

Per serving: Calories: 162, Protein: 7 gm., Carbohydrates: 18 gm., Fat: 8 gm.

CABBAGE PATCH SOUP

Yield: 6 servings

Place in a 3-quart pan and bring to a boil:

4 potatoes, cut in 1" chunks   **1 large onion, chopped**
4 cups water   **1 tsp. sea salt**

Reduce heat to low, simmer 15 minutes. Heat skillet and add:

2 Tbsp. safflower oil
½ head cabbage, chopped (4 cups)

Sauté 10 minutes, add to soup and simmer 5 minutes. With a slotted spoon, remove about a cup of the cooked potatoes to a soup bowl and mash with a fork. Stir mashed potato into soup to thicken it, stir in:

1 cup soymilk
¼ cup chopped parsley

Cook slowly a few minutes to heat milk but do no boil.

Per serving: Calories: 129, Protein: 4 gm., Carbohydrates: 18 gm., Fat: 5 gm.

LENTIL VEGETABLE SOUP

Yield: 8 servings

Combine in a soup pot:

2 cups brown lentils, washed,   **½ cup carrot, chopped**
**   drained**   **½ cup celery, chopped**
8 cups water   **2 cloves garlic, minced**
1 cup onion, chopped

Bring to a boil, lower heat, cover and simmer 1 hour. Add:

2 cups tomatoes (16 oz. can),   **2 Tbsp. brown rice vinegar**
**   chopped**   **   or apple cider vinegar**
¼ cup parsley, minced   **1 tsp. oregano**

Cook another 30 minutes.

Per serving: Calories: 127, Protein: 8 gm., Carbohydrates: 24 gm., Fat: 1 gm.

Variation: Add 2 Tempeh Breakfast Sausages (pg. 39), cooked and broken into pieces.

CALICO BEAN SOUP ☯

Yield: 6-8 servings

Rinse and soak 8 hours overnight:
> **2 cups mixed dried beans***

Drain, add:
> **6 cups water**
> **1 bay leaf**

Bring to a boil, reduce heat, cover and simmer 30 minutes.

Heat a skillet and add:
> **2 Tbsp. safflower oil**

Sauté:
> **1 large onion, chopped**
> **2 carrots, chopped**

Add to beans and simmer until beans are tender. Remove bay leaf.

Add:
> **½ tsp. garlic powder**
> **1 tsp. sea salt**
> **¼ tsp. cayenne**

*If your store doesn't have the calico mix, make your own with pintos, navy, pea, split peas, lentils, white limas, kidney, red and black beans.

Per serving: Calories: 186, Protein: 9 gm., Carbohydrates: 29 gm., Fat: 4 gm.

MISO WAKAME SOUP ☯

Yield: 4-6 servings

Place in a kettle:
> **4 cups water**

With scissors, cut into thin strips and add to pot:
> **12 inches wakame**

Bring to a boil, cover, reduce heat and simmer 15 minutes.
Add:
> **½ lb. tofu, cut in small cubes**
> **4 scallions or 1 cup watercress**

Pour a little soup into a bowl and dissolve:
> **3 Tbsp. dark miso**

Stir the miso into the soup, simmer for 1 minute only after miso is added, do not boil. Top each bowl with a slice of lemon or chopped scallions.

Per serving: Calories: 54, Protein: 5 gm., Carbohydrates: 4 gm., Fat: 2 gm.

BLACK BEAN SOUP ☯

Yield: 6 servings

Soak overnight or for 8 hours:
> **1½ cups black beans**

Drain beans. Add, and bring to a boil:
> **6 cups water**   **4" piece wakame or kombu**

Cover, simmer for 1 hour. Remove seaweed. Sauté:
> **1 Tbsp. olive oil**   **3 small carrots, cut chunky**
> **3 cloves garlic, smashed**   **2 stalks celery, sliced thinly**
> **2 small onions, cut in wedges**

When vegies are limp, add to beans and cook about 30 minutes until beans are tender. Stir in:
> **2 Tbsp. brown rice vinegar**   **2 tsp. cumin**
> **2 Tbsp. tamari**   **2 tsp. oregano**

Cook 10 minutes to blend flavors. Serve with a scoop of brown rice, if desired, garnish with chopped red onions.

Per serving: Calories: 149, Protein: 8 gm., Carbohydrates: 24 gm., Fat: 2 gm.

SUCCULENT
SALADS

● *Indicates macrobiotic recipe*

COLORFUL COUSCOUS SALAD

Yield: 8 servings

See photo opposite pg. 81.

Bring to a boil:
3 cups water

Stir in, cover and remove from heat:
2 cups couscous

Let sit 5 minutes, fluff with a fork, turn into large mixing bowl to cool.

Add:

**1 carrot, thinly sliced,
quartered
1 red pepper, chopped
½ cup almonds**

**¼ cup currants, soaked in 2
Tbsp. hot water
¼ cup chopped parsley
2 Tbsp. chopped red onion**

Blanch in boiling water:
½ cup almonds

Slip off skins, toast for 12 minutes at 350°. Cut into slivers, add to salad. Mix with dressing and serve.

For dressing, stir in a small bowl:

**juice of 1 lemon
½ cup olive oil
1 Tbsp. brown rice vinegar**

**2 tsp. brown rice syrup
1 tsp. dijon mustard
½ tsp. sea salt**

Stir dressing into salad.

Per serving: Calories: 338, Protein: 9 gm., Carbohydrates: 42 gm., Fat: 4 gm.

NUTTY RICE SALAD ☯

Yield: 6 servings

Have ready:
**2 cups cooked brown rice
½ cup cooked wheat berries**

Bring a quart of water to boiling, drop in:
**1 cup green string beans, slivered
1 carrot, cut in matchsticks**

Boil for 1½ minutes, drain and run cold water over to set color.

Combine with cooked grains and add:

¼ cup parsley, minced   **¼ cup green onions, chopped**
¼ cup chopped toasted walnuts

Serve on a bed of greens with Poppy Seed Dressing.

Per serving: Calories: 112, Protein: 3 gm., Carbohydrates: 18 gm., Fat: 3 gm.

POPPY SEED DRESSING

Yield: 6 servings

Combine in a jar, cover tightly and shake:

¼ cup safflower oil   **2 Tbsp. rice vinegar**
2 Tbsp. brown rice syrup   **2 tsp. poppy seeds**

Pour the dressing onto the salad and mix well. Serve at room temperature or chilled.

Per serving: Calories: 104, Protein: 0 gm., Carbohydrates: 5 gm., Fat: 10 gm.

CITRUS MOLDED SALAD

Yield: 8 servings

Peel fruit and section carefully, removing membranes from grapefruit. Cut up fruit and drain:

1 grapefruit, in sections   **2 navel oranges, in sections**

Bring to a boil:

1 cup grapefruit juice   **⅓ cup honey**
1 cup orange juice

Sprinkle with:

2 Tbsp. kanten flakes

Let dissolve, then cook 5 minutes, stirring. Pour into bowl to cool. When it begins to jell, stir in fruit and:

½ cup pecans, broken in pieces

Pour into mold, chill. To unmold, remove to room temperature and invert on a plate an hour before serving. Serve on salad greens with Tofu Mayonnaise (pg. 75).

Per serving: Calories: 186, Protein: 2 gm., Carbohydrates: 3 gm., Fat: 2 gm.

TOFU SALAD

Yield: 3½ cups

Drain, crumble into a bowl or grate coarsely:
> **1 lb. tofu**

Mix in:
> **½ cup chopped celery**
> **½ cup sweet red pepper, chopped**
> **¼ cup green onions, chopped fine**

Mix together, then stir into salad:
> **¼ cup oil**   **1 tsp. sea salt**
> **2 Tbsp. lemon juice**   **¼ tsp. tumeric**

Serve on lettuce with whole grain bread or crackers. Or use to stuff celery for an appetizer.

Per ½ cup serving: Calories: 125, Protein: 6 gm., Carbohydrates: 3 gm., Fat: 11 gm.

APPLE SALAD ☯

with Light Miso Dressing

Yield: 6 servings

A good choice for Thanksgiving dinner.

For dressing, shake up in a covered jar until well mixed:
> **3 Tbsp. light miso**   **1½ tsp. tamari**
> **1 Tbsp. sesame butter or**   **½ tsp. honey or brown rice**
> **tahini**   **syrup**
> **1 tsp. mirin**

For salad, mix together and chill:
> **3 large apples, chopped**   **¼ cup raisins**
> **1 cup celery, chopped**   **the dressing**
> **¼ cup walnuts**

Per serving: Calories: 132, Protein: 3 gm., Carbohydrates: 17 gm., Fat: 10 gm.

QUINOA SALAD ☯

Yield: 4 servings

The "mother grain" of the Incas, quinoa is actually a highly nutritious fruit, quick cooking with a light nutty flavor. It is one of the few grains that is a complete protein.

Rinse thoroughly and drain:
> **1 cup quinoa**

Place with 1¼ cups water, bring to a boil. Reduce heat, cover and simmer 10-15 minutes until liquid is absorbed. Turn onto plate to cool.

Mix with:
> **1 stalk celery, chopped** **¼ cup minced parsley**
> **1 carrot, chopped** **¼ cup small black olives**
> **¼ cup green onions, sliced**

Chill for an hour or more. Mix up for a dressing:
> **¼ cup olive oil** **1 tsp. basil**
> **¼ cup lemon juice** **2 cloves garlic, minced**

Serve on a bed of lettuce, garnished with wedges of tomato. Pour dressing over individual servings.

Per serving: Calories: 273, Protein: 6 gm., Carbohydrates: 24 gm., Fat: 5 gm.

CUCUMBERS with LEMON TAHINI

Yield: 6 servings

Peel and slice thinly:
> **2 cucumbers**

Combine in blender for dressing:
> **½ cup lemon juice** **2 Tbsp. tamari**
> **¼ cup tahini** **2 Tbsp. water**
> **2 Tbsp. oil** **½ tsp. celery seed**

Mix cucumbers and dressing, chill until serving time.

Per serving: Calories: 131, Protein: 3 gm., Carbohydrates: 6 gm., Fat: 18 gm.

CABBAGE SALAD ☯
with Umeboshi Dressing

Yield: 6 servings

Drop into a pot of lightly boiling water and boil 5 minutes:
a medium sized head of savoy or Chinese cabbage

Remove and drain while still firm and colorful, reserving a little of the cooking liquid for dressing. Cut up and spread out to cool quickly.

Mix in a suribachi for dressing:
½ cup chopped parsley	*2 tsp. lemon juice*
1 Tbsp. umeboshi paste	*1 tsp. toasted sesame oil*

Add enough cooking water to make creamy. Mix dressing with cabbage and let stand 10 minutes to develop flavors.

Per serving: Calories: 35, Protein: 3 gm., Carbohydrates: 5 gm., Fat: 1 gm.

HOT BROCCOLI and POTATO SALAD

Yield: 6 servings

Steam or cook in a small amount of boiling water until just tender:
5 new potatoes, medium size

Drain and keep warm.

Wash, peel stems and cut into bite-size pieces:
1 lb. broccoli

Steam stems and flower until crisp tender. Combine in a small pan, bring to a boil, then remove from heat:
¼ cup olive oil	*3 Tbsp. parsley, minced*
3 Tbsp. brown rice vinegar	*2 cloves garlic, minced*
2 Tbsp. mirin	*1 Tbsp. dried parsley*

Stir into dressing:
3 green onions, sliced with tops
¼ tsp. cayenne

Arrange potatoes and broccoli on a serving platter and pour hot mixture over them. Garnish with cherry tomatoes or parsley.

Per serving: Calories: 175, Protein: 5 gm., Carbohydrates: 20 gm., Fat: 2 gm.

66 SALADS

UDON NOODLE SALAD
with Sesame Dressing

Yield: 6 servings

Cook 10 minutes in boiling water, stirring occasionally, drain:
1-8 oz. pkg. udon noodles

Steam 5 minutes until crisp-tender:
½ lb. fresh green beans, cut in 2" lengths

Combine in a large bowl with:
½ cup cucumber, sliced
½ cup green onions, sliced
½ cup jicama or water chestnuts, chopped

Mix with Sesame Dressing. Cover and chill for several hours. Toss gently before serving.

For Sesame Dressing, shake up in a jar:

¼ cup sesame oil	**2 Tbsp. tamari**
2 Tbsp. lemon juice	**1 Tbsp. mirin**
1 Tbsp. toasted sesame seeds	**½ tsp. fresh ginger, grated**

Per serving: Calories: 247, Protein: 8 gm., Carbohydrates: 32 gm., Fat: 10 gm.

Tofu Noodle Salad: For a main dish salad, cut 1 lb. tofu into ½"
cubes. Mix 2 Tbsp. water, 2 Tbsp. lemon juice, 1 Tbsp. tamari and 1 tsp. minced raw ginger. Marinate tofu for 30 minutes. Sauté cubes in a little sesame oil until lightly browned. Add tofu cubes to salad just before serving.

ARTICHOKE PASTA SALAD

Yield: 6 servings

See photo between pgs. 80-1.

Cook and drain:
> **2 cups cooked sesame rice spirals or wheat rotini**

Steam for 2 minutes and cool:
> **2 cups raw broccoli flowers (bite-size)**
> **1 cup cauliflower (bite-size)**

Mix together, with noodles and:
> **1-14 oz. can artichoke hearts,**   **⅓-½ cup eggless mayonnaise**
> **drained**   **1 cup raw mushrooms, sliced**
> **½ cup chopped green onions**

Chill. Just before serving, garnish with slices of:
> **1 ripe avocado**

Per serving: Calories: 193, Protein: 10 gm., Carbohydrates: 32 gm., Fat: 5 gm.

Variation: You can substitute bottled Italian dressing or Lemon Vinaigrette Dressing (pg. 76) for the eggless mayonnaise.

PASTA SEA VEGETABLE SALAD
with Lemon Tahini Sauce

Yield: 6 servings

Cook about 10 minutes, until tender, drain:
> **½ lb. buckwheat noodles**

Steam 5 to 10 minutes, drain, cool:
> **2 cups steamed broccoli**
> **1 cup steamed asparagus**

Soak seaweed in water to cover 5 to 10 minutes, check for small pebbles:
> **1/8 to ¼ cup hijiki seaweed**

It will expand to 4 times original size. Saute briefly in a small amount of sesame oil with a dash of tamari. Mix with:
> **½ cup chopped green onions**   **¼ cup chopped carrots**
> **¼ cup chopped parsley**   **¼ cup chopped daikon (or**
> **radishes)**

Make the Lemon Tahini Sauce and mix all ingredients together. Serve chilled or at room temperature.

Per serving: Calories: 432, Protein: 15 gm., Carbohydrates: 37 gm., Fat: 53 gm.

Variation: Add 4 oz. tempeh, steamed for 10 minutes, cut into small cubes and marinated for 20 minutes in Shoyu Vinaigrette (pg. 130). Sauté in a little sesame oil and set aside to cool. Mix into salad with Lemon Tahini Sauce.

LEMON TAHINI SAUCE

Yield: 6 servings

Combine in a blender or beat well:

1 cup tahini	*½ tsp. cumin*
⅓ cup lemon juice	*Dash of cayenne*
¼ cup green onions	*Dash of paprika*
¼ cup minced parsley	*Dash of tamari*
1 clove garlic, minced	

The more you whip, the thicker it becomes. You can add water to thin it down.

Per serving: Calories: 301, Protein: 10 gm., Carbohydrates: 8 gm., Fat: 53 gm.

TACO SALAD

Yield: 4 large servings

Mix sauce and marinate tofu for 30 minutes or more:

1 lb. tofu, crumbled, drained	*¼ cup water*
¼ cup tamari	*2 Tbsp. peanut butter*
	¼ tsp. garlic powder

Oil a large skillet and brown tofu for about 10 minutes.

Combine in a large bowl:

1 head Boston or Bibb lettuce, torn up	*½ cup Thousand Island Dressing (pg. 75)*
2 tomatoes (in season), chopped	*¼ cup olives, chopped*
1 medium onion, chopped	*8 oz. salsa or picante sauce*
½ cup grated soy cheese	*6 oz. tortilla or blue corn chips, crumbled*

Toss tofu, chips, vegetables and sauces together, serve at once.

Per serving: Calories: 320, Protein: 17 gm., Carbohydrates: 22 gm., Fat: 15 gm.

PINE NUT SALAD
with Basil Dressing

Yield: 6 servings

Bring 2 cups water to a boil, add:

    1 ½ cups brown rice   *pinch of sea salt*

Reduce heat, cover and cook 35-45 minutes until liquid is absorbed. If rice begins to dry out before then, add a little more water.

Toast at 350° for 10 minutes:

    ½ cup pine nuts

Wash thoroughly, drain and chop:

    5 green onions, chopped   *1 red pepper, chopped fine*
    2 small carrots, cut in half moons

In blender or processor, puree for a dressing:

    ½ cup loosely packed fresh   *1 Tbsp. tamari*
      basil*   *2 Tbsp. lemon juice*
    ½ cup minced parsley   *2 Tbsp. mirin*
    ¼ cup olive oil   *2 cloves garlic, pressed*
    3 Tbsp. water

Mix rice, roasted pine nuts, onions and dressing in a salad bowl and serve at room temperature or chilled.

*If fresh basil is not available, use fresh parsley and add 2 Tbsp. crushed dried basil to dressing.

Per serving: Calories: 286, Protein: 5 gm., Carbohydrates: 32 gm., Fat: 9 gm.

CURRIED ALMOND RICE

Yield: 6 servings

Bring to a boil:

    3 cups water

Add:

    2 cups brown rice   *½ tsp. kelp or sea salt*

Cover, lower heat and simmer 40-45 minutes until water is absorbed. Turn out onto large platter to cool. Whisk together:

    ⅓ cup cider vinegar   *2 Tbsp. curry powder**

Add:

> *1 cup eggless mayonnaise*
> *1 cup tofu or non-dairy sour cream*

Mix warm rice and curry dressing and cool.

Blanch by dropping into boiling water for a few seconds, then slipping off the skins:

> *½ cup whole almonds*

Roast at 350° for 10 minutes. Sliver, add to rice with:

> *½ cup pitted green olives, cut in half*
> *½ cup pitted black olives, cut in half*

Cover and chill overnight if possible to develop flavors. Serve at room temperature garnished with chopped parsley.

*Curry powders vary in strength, with hot Madras powder you may prefer to use less.

Per serving: Calories: 436, Protein: 15 gm., Carbohydrates: 46 gm., Fat: 16 gm.

TABOULI (Bulgur Wheat)

Yield: 6 servings

Adding beans to a grain makes a complete protein meal.

Let soak for 30 minutes or until water is absorbed:

> *1 cup boiling water*
> *1 cup bulghur*

Stir in:

> *1 cup cooked chick peas*   *1 cucumber, chopped*
> *4 green onions, chopped*   *1 cup parsley, minced*
> *1 tomato, chopped*   *2 Tbsp. olive oil*
> *1 red pepper, chopped*   *juice of 1 lemon*
> *2 cloves garlic, minced*   *chopped fresh mint or basil*

Toss well and chill. Serve in pita pockets or on lettuce.

Per serving: Calories: 198, Protein: 6 gm., Carbohydrates: 32 gm., Fat: 5 gm.

Variation: Marinate chick peas ahead of time in a mixture of olive oil, minced red onion, brown rice vinegar and minced parsley. Let sit overnight.

TEMPEH PASTA SALAD

Yield: 6 servings

Steam for 10 minutes:
> *¼ lb. tempeh, cut into small cubes*

Marinate for 15 minutes in:
> *1 Tbsp. tamari*
> *2 Tbsp. water*
> *1 tsp. grated fresh ginger*

Heat **2 Tbsp. oil** and brown tempeh quickly. Cool on a paper towel.

Have ready:
> *8 oz. whole wheat spaghetti, cooked*
> *½ cup Tofu Mayonnaise (pg. 75)*
> *2 cloves garlic, minced*
> *1 green or red pepper, diced*

> *1 medium zucchini, sliced*
> *¼ lb. snow peas, blanched or raw*
> *2 Tbsp. brown rice vinegar*
> *1 tsp. curry powder*

Cut drained spaghetti strands into thirds. In a small bowl, whisk mayonnaise, garlic, vinegar and curry powder. Gently mix with pasta. Add other vegetables and cooked tempeh. If in season, garnish with cherry tomatoes, cut in half.

Mix:
> *¼ cup minced fresh basil*
> *½ cup fresh parsley*

Shower the salad with herbs, but do not toss. Serve at room temperature.

Per serving: Calories: 290, Protein: 14 gm., Carbohydrates: 35 gm., Fat: 11 gm.

RENEE'S WHEAT BERRY SALAD ☯

Yield: 6 servings

Bring to a boil in a large pot:
> *5 cups water*

Add:
> *pinch of sea salt*
> *2 cups wheat berries*

Cover, bring to a boil again, reduce heat and simmer 45 minutes to 1 hour, until wheat is tender. Set aside to drain and cool. Any leftover liquid can be used for tea or soupstock.

Add to berries:
> **4 scallions, chopped**
> **2 carrots, chopped**

Mix in a cup for dressing:

> **¼ to ½ cup olive or canola oil**
> **2 Tbsp. fresh minced parsley**
>
> **2 Tbsp. brown rice vinegar**
> **2 tsp. tamari**
> **1 tsp. thyme**

Mix dressing, taste salad and add a little sea salt if desired.

Per serving: Calories: 173, Protein: 4 gm., Carbohydrates: 2 gm., Fat: 13 gm.

Variation: Add ½ cup chopped yellow pepper, ¼ cup chopped red onion and ½ cup Jerusalem artichokes, chopped.

MARINATED CAULIFLOWER SALAD

Yield: 6 servings

Break *a head of cauliflower* into small pieces and drop into a kettle of boiling water with:
> **½ tsp. sea salt**
> **the juice of half a lemon (to keep the white color)**

Cook a few minutes, drain and cool. Combine in a salad bowl:

> **the drained cauliflower**
> **4 green onions, chopped**
> **2 carrots, cut in matchsticks**
>
> **1 red or green pepper, cut in matchsticks**
> **½ cup celery, sliced thinly**

Toss to moisten with:
> **¼ cup Lemon Vinaigrette Dressing (pg. 76)**

Per serving: Calories: 89, Protein: 3 gm., Carbohydrates: 8 gm., Fat: 1 gm.

ZUCCHINI SALAD ☯

Yield: 6 servings

Have ready in a bowl:
> **2 medium zucchini, sliced** **½ cup celery, sliced**
> **2 cups shredded cabbage** **¼ cup red onion, diced**

Cook in a small pan for just 1 minute:
> **¼ cup barley malt syrup** **2 tsp. celery seed**
> **¼ cup cider vinegar** **¼ tsp. sea salt**

Pour dressing over vegetables, toss and serve.

Per serving: Calories: 58, Protein: 2 gm., Carbohydrates: 14 gm., Fat: 0 gm.

TOMATO ASPIC

Yield: 6 servings

Bring to a boil:
> **2 cups tomato juice**
> **2 Tbsp. cider vinegar**
> **1 tsp. honey**

Sprinkle on top, let dissolve, then cook 3 minutes:
> **2 Tbsp. kanten flakes**

Pour into a bowl to cool. When it begins to jell, stir in:
> **½ cup diced celery**
> **½ cup sliced stuffed olives**

Pour into serving bowl. It will set at room temperature or can be chilled. To unmold, leave 1 hour at room temperature, then invert on plate. If made in a ring mold, fill center with tofu salad.

Per serving: Calories: 30, Protein: 1 gm., Carbohydrates: 5 gm., Fat: 1 gm.

TOFU MAYONNAISE ☯

Yield: 1¼ cups

Combine in a blender or food procesor and blend until creamy smooth:

½ lb. tofu, crumbled　　　**½ tsp. sea salt**
¼ cup oil　　　　　　　　　**pinch of cayenne**
3 Tbsp. lemon juice

This can be the base for delightful dips and other dressings.

Per 2 Tbsp. serving: Calories: 69, Protein: 2 gm., Carbohydrates: 1 gm., Fat: 7 gm.

Dill Dressing: Add 2 minced green onions and 2 tsp. dill weed.

Sesame Dressing: Add ½ tsp. garlic powder, 2 tsp. tamari and 1 Tbsp. toasted sesame seeds.

THOUSAND ISLAND DRESSING

Yield: 1½ cups

Add to *1 recipe for Tofu Mayonnaise* (pg. 75):

½ green pepper, chopped　　**1 Tbsp. parsley, finely**
small　　　　　　　　　　　　**chopped**
1 Tbsp. red onion, chopped　**2 Tbsp. Ketchup (pg. 128)**
small

If dressing is too thick to pour, thin with a little soymilk or water.

Per 2 Tbsp. serving: Calories: 59, Protein: 2 gm., Carbohydrates: 1 gm., Fat: 6 gm.

TOFU TAHINI DRESSING

Yield: 1½ cups

Combine in a blender or food processor:

½ lb. tofu　　　　　　　**2 Tbsp. water**
3 Tbsp. lemon juice　　**1 Tbsp. tamari**
2 Tbsp. tahini　　　　　**1 Tbsp. mirin**

Blend until creamy smooth. Chill for use on salad or fruit dishes.

Per 2 Tbsp. serving: Calories: 21, Protein: 1 gm., Carbohydrates: 1 gm., Fat: 4 gm.

SWEET SESAME DRESSING

Yield: 1 cup

Delicious with cold cooked grains.

Combine in a blender or food processor and blend until creamy smooth:

½ cup sesame tahini   **2 tsp. rice syrup or honey**
½ cup water   **2 tsp. lemon juice**
2 tsp. light miso

Per 2 Tbsp. serving: Calories: 119, Protein: 4 gm., Carbohydrates: 4 gm., Fat: 20 gm.

LEMON VINAIGRETTE

Yield: ⅔ cup

For herbs, use a mixture of tarragon, basil, dill or parsley.

Stir together:

3 Tbsp. lemon juice   **2 Tbsp. fresh herbs or 2 tsp.**
½ tsp. sea salt   **dried herbs**
¼ tsp. dry mustard

Slowly add:

½ cup olive oil

Keep in covered jar in refrigerator.

Per 1 Tbsp. serving: Calories: 88, Protein: 0 gm., Carbohydrates: .5 gm., Fat: 6 gm.

ENTICING ENTREES

● *Indicates macrobiotic recipe*

TOFU

BROCCOLI CASHEW STIR FRY

Yield: 6 servings

Cut into 2″ pieces:
> **2 cups broccoli flowers**

Have ready:
> **2 cups sliced carrots**

Bring to a boil:
> **1½ cups water**

Add:
> **pinch of sea salt**

Drop in the carrots and broccoli. Boil for 1 minutes. Drain and reserve the liquid for sauce.

Roast for 10 minutes at 350°:
> **1 cup cashew pieces**

Heat a wok or large skillet and over medium high heat, stir fry for 1 minute:
> **1 Tbsp. sesame oil**
> **1″ fresh ginger, minced**
> **2 onions, thinly sliced**

Add broccoli, carrots and cashews. Fry 2 minutes. Gently stir in:
> **1 lb. tofu, cut in cubes**
> **vegetable cooking liquid**

Cover pan, let steam 1 minute. Mix together:
> **2 Tbsp. arrowroot**
> **3 Tbsp. tamari**

Push vegetables to one side of the pan, add arrowroot and tamari to the juices. Let it boil up, then toss vegetables gently as sauce thickens. Serve over short or long grain rice or dry Chinese noodles.

Per serving: Calories: 259, Protein: 13 gm., Carbohydrates: 20 gm., Fat: 8 gm.

CHINESE FOO YUNG with TOFU

Yield: 8 servings

Have ready:
> **2 lbs. tofu**   **¼ cup tamari**

Reserve half a pound of tofu to crumble. Place other tofu in processor with tamari and blend until smooth. Blend in:
> **¾ cup whole wheat flour or whole wheat pastry flour**
> **2 tsp. baking powder**

Heat a skillet and stir fry over medium high heat:
> **2 Tbsp. light sesame oil**   **1 medium onion, chopped**
> **1 tsp. dark sesame oil**   **1 green pepper, chopped**
> **1 clove garlic, minced**   **1 cup celery, thinly sliced**
> **1 inch ginger, minced**

Stir in:
> **2 cups mung bean sprouts**
> **1-8 oz. can water chestnuts, chopped**

Combine the tofu mixture, the vegetables and the reserved tofu, mixing well. Preheat oven to 350°. Lightly oil a cookie sheet and shape 8 large round patties, leaving an inch of space between each round. Bake for 20 minutes, turn over and bake 10-15 more. Serve with Mushroom Gravy.

Per serving: Calories: 248, Protein: 12 gm., Carbohydrates: 18 gm., Fat: 8 gm.

MUSHROOM GRAVY

Yield: 8 servings

Heat a skillet and sauté for 2 minutes:
> **1 cup fresh mushrooms, diced**   **1 tsp. sesame oil**

Set mushrooms aside.

Mix and cook over medium heat until thick, whisking to avoid lumps:
> **2 cups cold water**   **2 Tbsp. arrowroot**

Add mushrooms to sauce and stir in:
> **2-3 Tbsp. tamari**

Cook until bubbling.

Per serving: Calories: 18, Protein: ½ gm., Carbohydrates: 3 gm., Fat: ½ gm.

CRUMB TOPPED BAKED VEGIES

Yield: 6 servings

Heat in a large skillet over medium heat and add:

2 Tbsp. sesame oil, light or   **2 Tbsp. fresh ginger, minced**
dark   **2 garlic cloves, chopped**
2 onions, sliced

Fry a few minutes, add:

2 medium carrots, sliced julienne
2 cups broccoli flowers, chopped

Cook 5 minutes, stir in:

2 cups kale, chopped
¼ cup water
2 Tbsp. tamari

Cover pan, reduce heat and simmer 10 minutes. Preheat oven to 350°.

For the topping, combine:

2 cups toasted whole grain   **1 Tbsp. basil**
bread cubes/crumbs   **1 Tbsp. oregano**
1 lb. tofu, mashed   **1 Tbsp. paprika**
¼ cup olive oil   **pinch of cayenne**

Place vegies in a 9" x 13" baking pan. Sprinkle evenly with topping and bake for 15-20 minutes.

Per serving: Calories: 297, Protein: 11 gm., Carbohydrates: 21 gm., Fat: 7 gm.

MARINATED BROILED TOFU

Yield: 6 servings

Cut crosswise to make 16 slices:
2 lbs. tofu

Combine in a covered jar and shake well:

½ cup tamari   **¼ cup lemon juice**
½ cup water   **3 tsp. grated fresh ginger**
½ cup minced onion   **1/8 tsp. cayenne**
¼ cup honey or ½ cup rice   **4 cloves garlic, finely**
syrup   **chopped**

Leek Shiitake Soup, pg. 56
Whole Wheat Croutons, pg. 44

Clockwise from left:
Baked Beans with Soysage, pg. 94
Rye Rolls with Caraway, pg. 46
Mother Nature's Apple Butter, pg. 126
Savoy Tofu Medley, pg. 82
Sesame Kombu, pg. 122

Clockwise from left:
Tamari Almonds, pg. 153
Fruit Kabobs, pg. 148
Carob Pecan Cookies, pg. 141
Carob Sunflower Balls, pg. 143
Artichoke Pasta Salad, pg. 68

Arrange tofu slices on a platter and saturate with marinade. Let soak in refrigerator 4 to 6 hours, turning every hour. Coat a cookie sheet with oil, arrange tofu slices. Broil 5 minutes on each side. Top tofu with chopped green onions. Serve with cooked grain or noodles.

Per serving: Calories: 131, Protein: 13 gm., Carbohydrates: 8 gm., Fat: 7 gm.

GINGER SESAME TOFU
with Spinach

Yield: 6 servings

Cut into small cubes:
1 lb. tofu

Place cubes in a 2 cup container that has a tight fitting lid.

Chop for marinade:
4 green onions, with tops   **1" fresh ginger**
2 cloves garlic

Add to vegetables:
¼ cup tamari   **2 tsp. honey**

Pour marinade over tofu cubes, cover container and let stand an hour or more, tipping container upside down from time to time so all the tofu is seasoned.

Rinse and trim off tough stems from:
2 lbs. fresh spinach or chard

Chop spinach or chard coarsely.

Heat in a large skillet or wok:
2 Tbsp. sesame oil
2 tsp. dark roasted sesame oil

Drain the tofu, saving any liquid. Put tofu, onions, garlic, ginger in skillet and stir fry a few minutes. Stir in spinach and the remaining marinade and cook a few minutes more.

Stir in, last:
¼ cup toasted sesame seeds

Serve over brown rice or with noodles.

Per serving: Calories: 194, Protein: 11 gm., Carbohydrates: 12 gm., Fat: 10 gm.

Colorful Couscous Salad, pg. 62

SPANISH TOFU CASSEROLE

Yield: 6 servings

Have ready:
> **3 cups cooked brown rice**

Heat skillet and sauté:
> **1 Tbsp. sesame oil**
> **2 cloves garlic, crushed**
> **2 medium onions, chopped**
>
> **2 stalks celery, chopped**
> **1 green pepper, chopped**

When vegetables are soft, stir in:
> **1 lb. tofu, diced**
> **2 cups tomatoes, chopped (a**
> **   16 oz. can)**
> **¼ cup black olives, chopped**
> **pinch of sea salt**
>
> **3 mild pepperocini peppers,**
> **   chopped**
> **2 Tbsp. tamari**
> **2 tsp. cumin**
> **2 tsp. chili powder**

Place half the cooked rice in the bottom of an oiled casserole, cover with the vegetable mixture. Spread rest of rice on top.

Pour over:
> **½ cup vegetable stock**

Sprinkle on top of casserole:
> **½ cup toasted cashews, chopped**

Bake at 325° for 30 minutes

Per serving: Calories: 284, Protein: 11 gm., Carbohydrates: 31 gm., Fat: 7 gm.

SAVOY TOFU MEDLEY

Yield: 6 servings

See photo between pgs. 80-81

Combine and parboil for 3 minutes:
> **2 carrots, sliced**
> **½ cup boiling water**
>
> **¼ cup raisins or currants**

Heat in a large skillet:
> **2 Tbsp. sesame oil**

Add and sauté about 10 minutes:

> **3 cups savoy cabbage, thinly**   **1 medium leek, sliced (opt.)**
> **sliced**
> **1 medium onion, sliced**

Combine with carrots and raisins. Mix together and add:

> **1 lb. tofu, cut in small cubes**

Mix together and stir in:

> **1 Tbsp. cider vinegar**
> **2 tsp. barley malt syrup**
> **½ tsp. sea salt**

Cover pan and simmer mixture about 5 minutes. Spoon into serving dish.

Sprinkle with:

> **2 Tbsp. fine bread crumbs (opt.)**

Per serving: Calories: 151, Protein: 7 gm., Carbohydrates: 15 gm., Fat: 8 gm.

TOFU MEATLESS LOAF

Yield: 6 servings

Crumble and mash:

> **1½ lbs. tofu**

Mix with tofu in a bowl:

> **1 cup whole grain bread**   **½ cup Ketchup (pg. 128)**
> **crumbs**   **2 Tbsp. dijon mustard**
> **½ cup rolled oats**   **½ tsp. garlic powder**
> **½ cup chopped black olives**   **½ tsp. thyme**
> **½ cup parsley, chopped fine**   **1 large onion, chopped fine**
>   **1 medium green pepper,**
>   **chopped fine**

Press into an oiled loaf pan. Bake at 350° for 1 hour. Let cool 10 minutes before removing from pan to slice.

Per serving: Calories: 273, Protein: 14 gm., Carbohydrates: 30 gm., Fat: 6 gm.

VEGETABLE CHOP SUEY

Yield: 6 servings

Cut into small cubes:
1 lb. tofu

Heat a wok or skillet, stir fry tofu in:
2 Tbsp. sesame oil

As an alternative, the cubes can be baked 30 minutes at 350°.

Remove tofu, add and stir fry over medium heat a few minutes:
1 Tbsp. sesame oil   **1" fresh ginger, grated**
1 medium onion, sliced   **2 cloves garlic, minced**

Add and stir fry:
½ cup cabbage, sliced

Add to pan, then cover and cook 5 minutes:
1 medium carrot, sliced   **1 stalk celery, thinly sliced**
thinly   **on the diagonal**
1 cup broccoli flowerets   **3 cups vegetable stock or**
1 green sweet pepper, diced **water**

Stir together:
2 Tbsp. arrowroot
¼ cup cold water

Add to vegetables and stir until thickened. Stir in:
2 Tbsp. tamari
1 cup mung bean sprouts
the browned tofu cubes

Serve over brown rice or Japanese soba or udon noodles.

Top with:
½ cup slivered almonds

Per serving: Calories: 226, Protein: 11 gm., Carbohydrates: 12 gm., Fat: 12 gm.

Variation: You can cut the calories in this recipe by a third replacing the almonds with sliced water chestnuts, cut in half and added to sauce.

MUSHROOM TOFU QUICHE

Yield: 6 servings

For the crust, toast in a dry skillet until it emits a nutty aroma:
> *½ cup millet flour (made in a blender or coffee grinder)*
> *½ cup corn meal*
> *½ cup whole wheat pastry flour*

Combine immediately with:
> *pinch of salt*
> *½ cup plus 2 Tbsp. water*

Stir with a fork to mix well. Press into an oiled 9″ pie pan with fingers. Bake shell at 350° for 5 minutes.

For the filling, heat skillet and sauté:
> *1 tsp. oil*
> *1 large onion, diced*
> *2 cloves garlic, minced*

Add and simmer 5 minutes:
> *¼ cup tamari*
> *2 tsp. thyme*

Have ready:
> *1½ lbs. tofu*

Grate half the tofu and set aside. Put remaining tofu in processor or blender, blend until smooth with:
> *2½ Tbsp. oil*
> *2 Tbsp. lemon juice*
> *2 Tbsp. water*

Have ready:
> *2 cups chopped kale or chard, steamed*
> *¼ cup parsley*
> *1 cup sliced, sautéed mushrooms*

Combine grated tofu, onions, mushrooms and chopped steamed greens. Mix in half of blended mixture. Pour into partially baked pie shell and spread remaining blended tofu over all. Bake at 350° for 35-40 minutes until firm.

Per serving: Calories: 289, Protein: 15 gm., Carbohydrates: 31 gm., Fat: 13 gm.

BROCCOLI SHIITAKE QUICHE ☯

Yield: 6 servings

Have ready:
> **1 single crust Whole Wheat Pie shell, (pg. 132)**
> **2-3 large shiitake mushrooms**

Prepare shiitake mushrooms by rinsing well, then pour warm water over them and let stand 15 minutes. Drain and chop. Prebake the crust for 10 minutes at 375°.

Heat a skillet and sauté:
> **2 Tbsp. sesame or sunflower
> oil**
> **2 cloves garlic, minced**
>
> **1 medium onion, chopped
> the chopped mushrooms**

After a few minutes, add:
> **½ cup chopped green onions**

Sauté a few minutes, then add to:
> **1½ lbs. tofu, mashed**

Mix in:
> **1 cup steamed broccoli
> flowers**
> **½ cup chopped black olives**
> **¼ cup chopped parsley**
>
> **1 Tbsp. tamari**
> **½ tsp. tumeric**
> **¼ tsp. each basil, rosemary
> and thyme**

Spoon into prebaked crust and bake at 350° for 30-40 minutes until firm. Cool a little before slicing.

Per serving: Calories: 306, Protein: 12 gm., Carbohydrates: 17 gm., Fat: 17 gm.

BEANS

HEARTY PINTO BEAN STEW

Yield: 6 servings

Rinse and soak overnight:
> *1 cup pinto beans*

Drain, add and bring to a boil:
> *5 cups water*
> *3" piece kombu*

Cover, reduce heat, simmer 1 hour until tender. Sauté together:
> *1 Tbsp. sesame oil*
> *2 onions, cut in large wedges*
> *2 tsp. fresh ginger, minced*

After 5 minutes, add:
> *2 carrots, cut in wedges*
> *1 parsnip, cut in chunks*

Sauté 5 minutes. Add vegetables to beans and cook until beans are tender. Remove 1 cup cooked beans, mash, stir in a little of the cooking liquid and:
> *2 Tbsp. dark miso*
> *1 Tbsp. light miso*

Stir well and return to pan. Let simmer 10 minutes, stirring occasionally. Mashed beans should give it a "gravy" consistency. Taste for seasonings. Serve on brown rice, garnish with minced parsley.

Per serving: Calories: 154, Protein: 7 gm., Carbohydrates: 27 gm., Fat: 2 gm.

CHICKPEAS with VEGETABLES

Yield: 4 servings

Rinse, soak overnight in water to cover:
> **1 cup chickpeas**

Add, and bring to a boil:
> **4 cups water**

Heat skillet, add oil and sauté onion until lightly browned.
> **1 large onion, sliced into wedges**
> **1 tsp. sesame oil**

Add to chickpeas with a pinch of sea salt, cover, reduce heat and simmer 1 to 1½ hours until tender. Drain excess liquid and save for soup stock.

For the sauce, heat pan, add oil and sauté until soft:
> **1 onion, sliced in wedges**
> **1 Tbsp. fresh ginger, minced**
> **2 tsp. sesame oil (toasted or plain)**

Add, with some of the cooking water from the beans:
> **1½ cups cauliflowerets**   **1 carrot, sliced**
> **½ cup broccoli flowers**

Cover and cook 10 minutes. Combine the cooked chickpeas with vegetables, simmer a few minutes. Gently stir in:
> **1 Tbsp. tamari**   **tsp. tahini**

Season to taste. Serve over rice or toast.

Per serving: Calories: 219, Protein: 11 gm., Carbohydrates: 30 gm., Fat: 8 gm.

LENTIL BULGHUR LOAF

Yield: 6 servings

Wash and drain:
> **1 cup lentils**

Combine in pan with:
> **3 cups water**   **1 tsp. oregano**
> **3" piece kombu**   **1 tsp. thyme**
> **1 bay leaf**

Bring to a boil, reduce heat, cover and simmer 35 minutes or until lentils are tender and liquid is absorbed. If lentils cook dry, add a little more water. If kombu doesn't disintegrate, remove, chop and return to pan.

In a small pan, bring to a boil:
> *1 cup water*

Stir in and simmer for 1 minute:
> *¾ cup bulghur*

Remove from heat, cover and let stand 20 minutes, until water is absorbed.

Sauté in skillet:
> *1 cup chopped onions*   *1 tsp. sesame oil*
> *½ cup chopped celery*   *3 cloves garlic, minced*

Mix together the cooked lentils, the bulghur, the sautéed vegetables and:
> *½ cup raw rolled oats*   *¼ cup minced parsley*
> *3 Tbsp. light miso,*   *juice of a half a lemon*
> *mixed with 1 Tbsp. water*

If you did not use kombu, season to taste with sea salt. Press into an oiled loaf pan, cover with foil. Bake at 350⁰ for 40 to 50 minutes. Let loaf rest for 15 minutes, then slice and serve with Miso Gravy.

Per serving: Calories: 263, Protein: 12 gm., Carbohydrates: 51 gm., Fat: 2 gm.

MISO GRAVY ☯

Yield: 6 servings

Sauté in a sauce pan:
> *1½ Tbsp. olive oil*   *1 clove garlic, minced*
> *1 onion, diced*

Reduce heat, add and stir for 1 minute:
> *3 Tbsp. whole wheat flour*

Add and cook until gravy thickens and bubbles:
> *1½ cups water*

Combine, then stir into gravy:
> *3 Tbsp. light miso*   *½ cup water*

Add and simmer 5-10 minutes:
> *1 Tbsp. mirin*   *¼ cup minced parsley*

Per serving: Calories: 71, Protein: 2 gm., Carbohydrates: 9 gm., Fat: 1 gm.

SPICY LENTIL PATTIES ☯

Yield: 12 patties

Rinse lentils and combine:
1 cup lentils   **3 cups water**

Bring to a boil, reduce heat, add:
1 tsp. curry powder   **1 tsp. coriander**
pinch sea salt   **1 tsp. cumin**

Cover pan and cook 35-45 minutes until tender. Set aside, with lid on.

Heat a skillet and sauté:
¼ cup carrot, chopped fine   **1 large onion, chopped**
2 cloves garlic, chopped   **2 tsp. olive oil**

Lentils should absorb remaining liquid, or drain them. Mash lentils, mix with sautéed vegetables and:
1½ cups whole grain bread crumbs

Crumbs can be made by putting broken pieces of bread into blender and blend a few seconds.

Mix in:
2 Tbsp. arrowroot
2 Tbsp. tomato paste, mixed with 1 Tbsp. light miso

Form into balls and flatten into patties. Place on an oiled baking sheet in a 350° oven. Bake 20 minutes, turn over and bake 20 minutes more. These can be served in Healthy Burger Buns (pg. 47).

Per serving: Calories: 112, Protein: 5 gm., Carbohydrates: 21 gm., Fat: ½ gm.

CHICKPEAS and CARROT SAUCE ☯

Yield: 4 servings

Rinse, sort and soak overnight:
1 cup chickpeas

Rinse, bring to a boil with:
3 cups water

Cover, reduce heat and simmer 1 to 1½ hours, until tender.

Heat a 2 quart pan and sauté:

2 carrots, cut in chunks   **1 Tbsp. sesame oil**
1 large onion, cut in wedges   **1 Tbsp. fresh ginger, chopped**
                                    fine

Remove half the chickpeas to a bowl and mash. Add to onions, with remaining chickpeas and the cooking liquid. Cover and simmer until vegetables are tender.

Stir in:

2 Tbsp. arrowroot, dissolved in ¼ cup cold water
pinch of sea salt

Cook, stirring until thickened. Blend in:
1 Tbsp. tamari   **½ cup chopped parsley**

Serve over couscous or rice.

Per serving: Calories: 189, Protein: 8 gm., Carbohydrates: 28 gm., Fat: 4 gm.

CURRIED LENTILS
with Condiments

Yield: 4 servings

Double this recipe for a company dish. See photo opposite pg. 128.

Rinse lentils and cook 35-40 minutes until soft:
1 cup lentils   **5 cups water**

Sauté for 2 minutes:

1 Tbsp. sesame or sunflower   **½ cup celery, chopped**
oil   **2 cloves garlic, minced**
1½ cups onions, chopped

Add and cook until soft:

2 Tbsp. barley malt or 1   **½ tsp. ground coriander**
Tbsp. honey   **¼ tsp. cayenne**
2 tsp. curry powder
1 tsp. chili powder

Drain lentils and add stock to vegetables, simmer 5 minutes. Add lentils and simmer 10 minutes. Serve over brown rice or couscous with side dishes of raisins, coconut, chopped green onions, sliced banana, chopped peanuts and Ginger Pear Chutney (pg. 127).

Per serving: Calories: 191, Protein: 10 gm., Carbohydrates: 32 gm., Fat: 4 gm.

SMITH VALLEY FARMS VEGIE PIE

Yield: 6 servings

For crust, mix together:

2½ cups cooked brown rice
¼ cup soy parmesan cheese (opt.)
2 tsp. tamari

2 tsp. toasted sesame oil
1 tsp. egg replacer in 1 Tbsp. water
¼ tsp. garlic powder

Lightly coat a 9″ pie pan with oil. Fill with brown rice mixture and press down on bottom and sides of pan.

For filling, place in pie shell:

2½ cups chopped broccoli, steamed
½ cup chopped black olives

¼ cup whole kernel corn
2 Tbsp. soaked, chopped arame

Mix in a small sauce pan:

¾ cup soymilk
1 Tbsp. arrowroot

2 tsp. tamari
pinch of sea salt

Heat, stirring until thickened. Pour over vegetables, top with:

1 cup grated soy mozzarella

Bake at 350° for 30 minutes, until crust turns lightly brown. Let cool for 5 minutes before serving.

Per serving: Calories: 239, Protein: 8 gm., Carbohydrates: 25 gm., Fat: 7 gm.

SPLIT PEA STEW ☯
and Brown Rice

Yield: 10-12 servings

Combine in a soup pot:

8 cups water
1 cup brown rice, rinsed

1 cup green split peas, rinsed
½ cup red split peas

Bring to a boil, cover, reduce heat and simmer 20 minutes.

Steam:

½ lb. tempeh, cut in small cubes

Heat a skillet, add:

2 tsp. olive oil

Sauté tempeh to brown quickly, adding:

2 tsp. tamari

Remove tempeh, heat pan and sauté 5 minutes:

1 tsp. olive oil
1 carrot, cut in chunks

1 large onion, cut in wedges

Add vegetables to rice and peas, along with:

1½ cups cubed, cooked butternut squash
juice of 2 lemons

When rice is cooked, dissolve and add:

¼ cup light miso
¼ cup water

Cook over low heat 10 minutes more. Stir in the tempeh cubes. Stew should be thick, with most of liquid absorbed. If necessary, add water when reheating leftovers.

Per serving: Calories: 212, Protein: 11 gm., Carbohydrates: 33 gm., Fat: 3 gm.

BAKED BEANS WITH SOYSAGE

Yield: 8-10 servings

An economical and healthy way to feed a crowd. See photo between pgs. 80-1.

Wash and soak overnight:
> **1 cup navy beans**   **1 cup pinto beans**

Drain, add:
> **6 cups fresh water**
> **1 bay leaf**   **1 tsp. kelp**

Cover, bring to a boil, reduce heat and cook 1½ to 2 hours until beans are tender. Remove bay leaf. Meanwhile, cook:
> **3 cups water**   **1 tsp. sea salt**
> **1½ cups brown rice**

Heat a skillet and add:
> **½ cup celery, chopped**   **2 cloves garlic, chopped**
> **2 Tbsp. safflower oil**   **1 large onion, chopped**

When onions are soft, stir in:
> **¼ cup molasses**   **14 oz. pkg. of soysage, cut**
> **1 tsp. thyme**   **into small cubes**
> **1 tsp. sage**

Cook a few minutes, then combine with the cooked brown rice, and the drained cooked beans. Taste for seasonings and add a little sea salt if desired. Put in an oiled bean pot or covered casserole, cover and bake at 350° for 1 hour.

Per serving: Calories: 376, Protein: 18 gm., Carbohydrates: 47 gm., Fat: 12 gm.

BLACK BEAN and VEGETABLE STEW

Yield: 4 servings

Wash and sort, discarding any shrivelled beans:
> **1 cup black beans**

Soak beans overnight, drain, combine with:
> **4 cups water**   **3″ piece kombu**

Bring to a boil, reduce heat, cover and simmer 1 hour, until partly tender. Add 1 to 2 cups more water if needed. Add:
> **2 stalks celery, sliced**   **2 potatoes, chunked**
>   **2 carrots, sliced**

Heat a skillet and sauté:

2 Tbsp. sesame oil　　　　　　**1 cup onion, chopped**
3 cloves garlic, chopped　　　　**1" fresh ginger, chopped**

Add sautéed vegetables to beans, with:

2 Tbsp. tamari　　　　　　　　**juice of 1 lemon**
¼ cup parsley　　　　*arsley*

Serve over brown rice or millet.

Per serving: Calories: 224, Protein: 9 gm., Carbohydrates: 33 gm., Fat: 8 gm.

BLACK BEAN NACHOS

Yield: 6 servings

Great on blue corn chips.

Wash well, removing any shrivelled beans or stones:
2 cups black beans

Soak in water overnight. Drain, combine with:
3 quarts water　　　　　　　**1 bay leaf**

Bring to a boil, cover, reduce heat and simmer until beans are tender (about 1½ hours). Or pressure cook in 1 quart water for 35 minutes. Remove one cup of beans and puree or mash to thicken sauce.

Heat oil in a skillet and sauté:
2 jalapeno peppers, finely　　**1 large onion, chopped**
**　　chopped**　　　　　　　　　**¼ cup olive oil**

Add:
1 Tbsp. cider vinegar　　　　**2 tsp. oregano**
2 tsp. cumin　　　　　　　　**1 tsp. sea salt**

Add the pureed beans, remaining cooked beans and a little bean liquid if needed. Place on a large platter:
14 oz. pkg. nacho chips

Pour beans over chips and top with:
½ cup chopped red onion

Garnish with avocado slices or grated soy mozzarella cheese.

Per serving: Calories: 256, Protein: 9 gm., Carbohydrates: 29 gm., Fat: 5 gm.

TEMPEH

BAKED TEMPEH with KALE

Yield: 4 servings

Steam for 10 minutes, set aside:
½ lb. tempeh, defrosted

Heat pan, and sauté until tender:
1 Tbsp. sesame oil   **2 cloves garlic, chopped**
2 onions, chopped   **1 carrot, chopped**

Stir in until vegetables are coated:
¼ cup whole wheat flour
¼ cup nutritional yeast

Stir in, a little at a time:
2 cups water

Keep stirring as sauce thickens. After mixture bubbles, add:
2-3 Tbsp. tamari

Cut tempeh into 1″ cubes. Add to sauce, with:
2 cups kale, chopped, steamed

Pour into a lightly oiled casserole dish. Bake at 350° for 20 minutes. Serve with millet or couscous.

Per serving: Calories: 244, Protein: 16 gm., Carbohydrates: 21 gm., Fat: 9 gm.

TEMPEH MUSHROOM STROGANOFF

Yield: 6 servings

Cut into small cubes and steam for 10 minutes:
1 lb. tempeh

Heat a skillet and sauté tempeh to quickly brown in:
1 Tbsp. sesame oil

Remove tempeh from pan. Add and sauté:
>   *1 Tbsp. sesame oil*
>   *1 large onion, chopped*
>   *¾ lb. mushrooms, sliced*

Mix together and stir into pan:
>   *½ cup cold water or soymilk*
>   *2 Tbsp. arrowroot*

Cook a few minutes to thicken. Dissolve and add:
>   *2 Tbsp. light miso*
>   *2 Tbsp. dark miso*
>   *1 cup water or vegetable broth*

Stir into sauce:
>   *1 tsp. oregano*
>   *½ tsp. thyme*
>   *¼ tsp. cayenne*

Return tempeh to pan. If too thick, add a little water.

Add and gently heat but do not boil:
>   *1 cup Soymilk Sour Cream (pg. 97)*

Serve over noodles or rice.

Per serving: Calories: 255, Protein: 18 gm., Carbohydrates: 16 gm., Fat: 12 gm.

SOYMILK SOUR CREAM

Yield: 1 cup

Combine in blender at low speed:
>   *½ cup cold soymilk**   *¼ tsp. sea salt*
>   *½ tsp. onion powder*   *¼ tsp. garlic powder*

Add slowly at high speed:
>   *¼ cup sesame oil*

Blend in on high:
>   ⅓ cup lemon juice

*You can make soymilk by combining 1 Tbsp. instant soy powder and ½ cup water.

Per ¼ cup serving: Calories: 138, Protein: 1 gm., Carbohydrates: 2 gm., Fat: 15 gm.

GRAINS

BROWN RICE ☯

Yield: 4 ¼ cups

One cup uncooked rice makes about 2 cups cooked.

Wash several times or until water is clear:
> **2 cups short grain brown rice**

Combine in a pan with:
> **2½ cups water**
> **1 pinch sea salt for each cup rice**

Using high heat, bring to a boil, then reduce heat to simmer and cover pot. Cook 30 minutes, then check to see if the liquid has been absorbed and the rice is tender. If not, cook 10 to 15 minutes more, checking occasionally. Stir gently after rice is cooked.

To pressure cook:
Bring water and rice to a boil over high heat to 15 lbs. pressure. Let the regulator jiggle hard for 1 minute, then reduce heat to low (regulator will rock briefly every minute or so) and cook 20 minutes. Let the pressure come down naturally.

Per ½ cup serving: Calories: 76, Protein: 2 gm., Carbohydrates: 16 gm., Fat: 0 gm.

WILD GRAIN PILAF ☯

Yield: 6 servings

Have ready:
> **½ cup wheat berries**   **¼ cup wild rice**
> **1 cup short grain brown rice**   **½ tsp. anise seed**
>   **4¼ cups vegetable stock**

Soak wheat berries in water to cover for 3 to 4 hours. Drain. Mix the brown rice, wild rice, berries and anise seed in a medium-sized saucepan. Add the stock. Cover, bring to a boil, reduce heat and simmer gently 40-45 minutes. Remove from heat and let stand until liquid is absorbed, about 15 minutes.

Sauté:
> **1 Tbsp. olive oil**   **¼ cup green onions, chopped**
> **2 garlic cloves, chopped**   **2 celery stalks, diced**
> **½ cup onion, chopped**

When soft, add and cook 3 minutes:
> ½ cup mushrooms, sliced

Sprinkle vegetables with:
> ½ tsp. chili powder   pinch of cayenne
> 1 tsp. cumin

When grains are tender, mix with vegetables and:
> ¼ cup pine nuts, toasted   2 Tbsp. cilantro, chopped

Turn into a bowl and serve.

Per serving: Calories: 269, Protein: 8 gm., Carbohydrates: 48 gm., Fat: 4 gm.

VEGETABLE PIZZA with Whole Wheat Crust

Yield: 6 servings

Mix together for crust:
> 1 Tbsp. dry yeast   ¼ cup warm water

Let stand for 5 minutes, then add:
> ¾ cup water   1½ cups whole wheat flour
> 2 Tbsp. olive oil   1½ cups whole wheat pastry
> ¼ cup cornmeal   flour
> ¼ cup sesame seeds   ¼ cup mashed tofu (opt.)

Knead dough for 5 minutes until smooth and elastic. Cover and let rise 1 hour. Oil a cookie sheet and roll out pizza dough onto sheet. Push sides up for edges of crust.

Spread lightly with:
> a little olive oil
> a thin layer your favorite tomato sauce

Or use the Tomato-less Spaghetti Sauce (pg. 106)

Sprinkle with:
> 1 tsp. each basil and oregano

Sauté for 5 minutes:
> 1 Tbsp. olive oil   1 sliced green pepper
> 2 sliced onions   1 cup mushrooms

Spread vegetables on top of pizza. Add chopped black olives if desired, or browned tempeh or tofu cubes. Top with grated soy mozzarella cheese if desired. Heat oven to 400° and bake pizza for 20-25 minutes.

Per serving: Calories: 358, Protein: 11 gm., Carbohydrates: 53 gm., Fat: 3 gm.

KASHA

Yield: 4 servings

You can buy toasted buckwheat groats or toast washed buckwheat in a dry skillet for a few minutes, shaking the pan.

Place the toasted grain in a medium pot:
> **1 cup buckwheat groats**

Add, bring to a boil, cover, lower heat and simmer 20-30 minutes:
> **2 cups boiling water**   **pinch of sea salt**

Sauté together:
> **1 Tbsp. sesame oil**   **1 cup cabbage, chopped**
> **¼ cup chopped onion**

Mix vegetables with cooked kasha. Serve garnished with:
> **chopped green onions and parsley**

Per serving: Calories: 261, Protein: 8 gm., Carbohydrates: 49 gm., Fat: 5 gm.

BARLEY PILAF

Yield: 4 servings

Simmer for 1 hour:
> **3 cups vegetable stock or**   **1 cup barley**
> **water**   **¼ tsp. sea salt**

Sauté until tender:
> **1 Tbsp. sesame oil**   **½ cup green onion, sliced**
> **1 onion, sliced**   **5 shiitake mushrooms,**
> **1 carrot, chopped**   **soaked, drained and sliced**
> **1 stalk celery, chopped**

Stir vegetables into the cooked barley, adding:
> **1 Tbsp. tamari**   **1 tsp. thyme**

Simmer the pilaf for 5 minutes, until liquid is absorbed.

Serve with:
> **fresh parsley or kale for garnish**

Per serving: Calories: 234, Protein: 6 gm., Carbohydrates: 45 gm., Fat: 4 gm.

100 ENTREES

BROWN RICE CASHEW LOAF

Yield: 6 servings

Toast in a dry skillet for 5-10 minutes:
>   *1½ cups raw cashews*

Remove nuts and chop. Sauté about 5 minutes:
>   *1 Tbsp. oil*
>   *2 cups onions, chopped*
>   *1 cup celery, chopped*

Mix nuts and onions with:

>   *2 cups cooked brown rice*   *1 tsp. sage*
>   *2 Tbsp. tamari*   *3 slices whole grain bread,*
>   *1 cup soymilk or vegetable*   *cubed*
>   *stock*   *¼ cup chopped parsley*
>   *1 cup water*   *1 tsp. thyme*

When ingredients are well mixed, pack in an oiled covered baking dish or loaf pan and cover with foil. Bake at 350° for one hour. Remove cover the last 30 minutes of cooking. Serve with Country Style Gravy.

Per serving: Calories: 339, Protein: 10 gm., Carbohydrates: 35 gm., Fat: 6 gm.

COUNTRY STYLE GRAVY

Yield: 6 servings

Liquefy in a blender:

>   *2 cups water*   *1 Tbsp. sesame oil*
>   *½ cup cashews*   *1 tsp. tamari*
>   *2 Tbsp. arrowroot or 3 Tbsp.* *2 tsp. onion, minced*
>   *browned flour*   *¼ tsp. celery seed*

Pour into a saucepan and stir until thick. Serve with Brown Rice Cashew Loaf.

Per serving: Calories: 96, Protein: 2 gm., Carbohydrates: 6 gm., Fat: 3 gm.

NUTTY BROWN RICE
with Red Bean Sauce

Yield: 4 servings

Bring to a boil:
> **1 cup brown rice, rinsed**
> **2 cups water**
> **pinch sea salt**

Reduce heat, cover and simmer for 45-50 minutes until liquid is absorbed and rice is tender. (A flame tamer placed under the pot will keep grains from burning.)

Set aside to cool slightly. In a bowl, combine rice with:

> **½ cup sliced green onions**   **½ tsp. dried basil, crushed**
> **½ cup walnuts, chopped**   **½ tsp. dried thyme, crushed**
> **¼ cup dry bread crumbs**
> **pinch of cayenne**

For sauce, cook until soft:
> **2 Tbsp. sesame oil**
> **¼ cup onion, chopped**

Stir in:
> **2 cups cooked red kidney beans (undrained)**
> **1 tsp. chili powder**

When beans are hot, stir in:
> **2 Tbsp. miso (dark or light) diluted in 1 cup water**

Simmer, uncovered, 3 minutes or until heated through. Mash slightly. Spoon over a mound of rice mixture and, if desired, top with:
> **shredded soy cheese**

Per serving: Calories: 460, Protein: 16 gm., Carbohydrates: 62 gm., Fat: 16 gm.

MOCHI VEGETABLE MELT

Yield: 4 servings

Heat oil in a heavy skillet and sauté:
> **2 Tbsp. sesame oil**   **1 onion, chopped**
> **1 cup kale, chopped fine**   **½ cup green cabbage,**
> **chopped**

Add:

> **3 carrots, sliced**

Cover and cook over medium heat for 10 minutes. Stir in:

> **2 Tbsp. tamari**

Reduce heat. Cut into 1″ squares and place on top of vegetables:

> **½ of 8 oz. pkg. of mochi**

Cover and cook slowly another 10 to 15 minutes until the mochi absorbs the juices of the vegetables, softens and melts into the vegetable mixture.
Add:

> **½ lb. tofu, cubed and sautéed**

Per serving: Calories: 205, Protein: 9 gm., Carbohydrates: 30 gm., Fat: 7 gm.

OAT MUSHROOM BURGERS

Yield: 20 patties

Sauté until soft:

> **2 Tbsp. sesame or corn oil**   **¾ lb. fresh mushrooms, diced**
> **1½ cups onion, diced small**
> **½ cup carrots, diced small**

Bring to a boil in a 2-quart pan:

> **4 cups water or vegetable stock**

Add sautéed vegetables and:

> **¼ cup tamari**   **1 tsp. oregano**
> **⅓ cup nutritional yeast**   **1 tsp. thyme**
> **2 cloves garlic, minced**   **½ tsp. marjoram**

Add 1 cup at a time, letting oats sink in, then stirring:

> **5 cups rolled oats**

Cook for 5 minutes until mixture is thick at the bottom of the pot. Cover, set aside for 15 minutes, as it continues to thicken. Cool and shape into patties. Place on an oiled cookie sheet. Bake at 350° for 45 minutes, turning after 20 minutes. Serve hot in buns or cold in sandwiches with lettuce and mayonnaise.

Per patty: Calories: 116, Protein: 10 gm., Carbohydrates: 27 gm., Fat: 4 gm.

STUFFED BUTTERNUT SQUASH ☯

Yield: 4 servings

Cut in half, scoop out seeds from:
> **2 butternut squash (1 lb. each)**

Rub a little olive oil on the inside flesh.

Heat in a 2-quart pan:
> **1 Tbsp. olive or sesame oil**

Sauté gently until softened:
> **1 cup onion, chopped**   **2 cloves garlic, crushed**

Add to pan:
> **1½ cups bulghur wheat,**   **¼ cup green onion, chopped**
> **washed and drained**   **¼ tsp. nutmeg**
> **1¼ cups warm water**   **¼ tsp. ground cloves**
> **1 red pepper, diced**

Cook over low heat, stirring occasionally, about 10 minutes. Add a little more water if needed.

Stir in:
> **½ cup walnuts, chopped**

Preheat oven to 400°. Fill squash halves with bulghur mixture, place in lightly oiled baking pan. Bake 45 minutes to 1 hour, until squash is tender. Pour Miso-Walnut Sauce over squash before serving.

Per serving: Calories: 59, Protein: 15 gm., Carbohydrates: 19 gm., Fat: 5 gm.

MISO-WALNUT SAUCE ☯

Yield: 1 cup

Place in a food processor or blender:
> **½ cups walnuts**   **3 cloves garlic, cut up**

Process until nuts are ground, add:
> **½ cup water**   **2 tsp. light miso**
> **3 Tbsp. olive oil**   **juice of 1 lemon**
> **2 Tbsp. whole wheat bread-**
> **crumbs**

Add a little water if too thick. Serve over Stuffed Butternut Squash, steamed vegetables or a baked loaf.

Per ¼ cup serving: Calories: 205, Protein: 4 gm., Carbohydrates: 5 gm., Fat: 10 gm.

VEGETARIAN CHILI
with Bulghur

Yield: 8 servings

Rinse, pick over and soak overnight:
> **2 cups kidney beans**
> **½ cup pinto beans**

Rinse beans, bring to a boil with:
> **7 cups water**
> **3" piece kombu**

Reduce heat, cover and cook 1 to 1½ hours until soft. If kombu does not disintegrate, chop and return to pan.

Heat a large pan and sauté:
> **2 Tbsp. olive oil**   **1 cup celery, chopped**
> **3 cloves garlic, crushed**   **1½ cup carrots, chopped**
> **1½ cups onion, chopped**

When onions, are almost tender add:
> **½ cup green pepper, chopped**

Cook a few minutes more. Add:
> **2 cups tomato sauce**   **2 tsp. basil**
> **1 cup fresh tomato, chopped**   **1 tsp. chili powder**
> **juice of 1 lemon**   **1 tsp. thyme**
> **2 tsp. ground cumin**   **¼ tsp. cayenne**

Add:
> **the cooked beans**
> **1 cup raw bulghur**

Cook slowly for 10 minutes. Serve with Mexican Corn Bread (pg. 43) and a green salad.

Per serving: Calories: 410, Protein: 17 gm., Carbohydrates: 77 gm., Fat: 1 gm.

PASTA

TOMATO-LESS SPAGHETTI SAUCE

Yield: 6 servings

Dice:
> ***½ cup beets***

Chop:
> ***the beet greens***

Steam for 20 minutes or until tender:
> ***the beets***   ***1 green pepper, diced***
> ***4 stalks celery, sliced***   ***the beet greens***
> ***4 carrots, sliced***   ***1 cup warm water***

Heat a pan, sauté:
> ***3 cloves garlic, minced***   ***2 Tbsp. olive oil***
> ***2 large onions, chopped***

Add to vegetables and mash or puree in blender. Dissolve:
> ***3 Tbsp. dark miso***
> ***½ cup warm water***

Add to vegetables with:
> ***½ cup warm water***   ***1 tsp. oregano***
> ***2 Tbsp. tamari***   ***1 tsp. basil***
> ***2 Tbsp. mirin***   ***pinch of cayenne***

Simmer sauce 5 minutes. Serve over whole wheat spaghetti or buckwheat noodles.

Per serving: Calories: 130, Protein: 4 gm., Carbohydrates: 14 gm., Fat: 2 gm.

VEGETARIAN LASAGNE

Yield: 6 servings

Soak for 15-20 minutes in cold water:
>   *1 cup Italian-flavored LumenXTM or ½ cups textured vegetable protein (TVP), soaked in ½ cup boiling water*

Drain. Cook according to package directions:
>   *½ lb. whole wheat lasagna noodles*

Drain, keep warm. Mash in a large bowl:
>   *1½ lbs. firm tofu*
>   *2 cloves garlic, chopped*
>   *1 onion, chopped*

Soak in warm water to cover for 10 minutes:
>   *4 shiitake mushrooms*

Remove, chop add to tofu with:
>   *½ lb. kale, steamed, chopped*   *½ tsp. basil*
>   *1 tsp. oregano*   *½ tsp. thyme*

Have ready:
>   *1-32 oz. jar tomato sauce*
>   *2 cups steamed broccoli*

Begin layering: place 3 noodles on the bottom of a lightly oiled 9" x 13" pan. Spread on a third of the tofu mixture. Cover with half the tomato sauce, the broccoli and some pieces of lumen or TVP. Continue layering noodles, tofu mixture, lumen and sauce, ending with noodles. Sprinkle on top:
>   *¼ cup sunflower seeds, toasted*

Or, if desired, top with:
>   *2 cups grated soy cheese (opt.)*

Preheat oven to 350° and bake lasagne for 30 minutes.

Per serving: Calories: 322, Protein: 22 gm., Carbohydrates: 55 gm., Fat: 2 gm.

Variation: Substitute Dairy-less Seed Cheese (pg. 130) for the tofu to get a cheese flavor with a consistency of ricotta cheese.

PASTA PRIMAVERA ☯
with Garden Green Sauce

Yield: 6 servings

Cut flowerets from
1 small bunch broccoli (2-3 cups)

Wash and drain flowers, set aside. Peel the broccoli stems, cut into small pieces. Steam pieces in a small amount of water for 5 minutes. Save the cooking liquid, adding enough water, if necessary, to make 1 cup. Set aside.

Heat sauce pan and sauté:
½ cup onion, chopped
2 cloves garlic, minced
2 tsp. olive oil

Add and bring to a boil:
1 cup cooking liquid

Add stems, simmer 2 minutes. Add:
1 Tbsp. arrowroot dissolved in
2 Tbsp. water

Simmer a few minutes. Stir in:
1½ cups chopped parsley or cilantro
1 green onion, chopped

Combine in a bowl:
¼ lb. tofu, crumbled   1 Tbsp. chopped basil (prefer-
2 Tbsp. light miso   ably fresh)
1 Tbsp. mirin   1 tsp. oregano

Combine greens and tofu mixture and puree in a processor or blender. Keep sauce warm.

Sauté for about 3 minutes:
5 fresh or soaked and   1 tsp. sesame oil
drained dried shiitake   1 tsp. tamari
mushrooms

Have ready:
2 carrots, cut in matchsticks
the broccoli flowerets

Bring 5 cups of water to a boil. Drop in broccoli flowerets and cook 2 minutes, remove, run under cold water to set color. Drop carrot sticks into boiling water and blanch for 2 minutes, remove with slotted spoon. Cook 2 minutes, drain, reserve liquid for soup stock.

Cook until tender and arrange on a platter:
> *1-8 oz pkg. buckwheat or angel hair pasta*

Top with green sauce, then arrange vegetables on top. Sprinkle with:
> *½ cup pine nuts, roasted*

Per serving: Calories: 270, Protein: 10 gm., Carbohydrates: 62 gm., Fat: 8 gm.

MISO PESTO and LINGUINE

Yield: 4 servings

Most pestos are made with parmesan cheese. In this recipe miso is used instead.

Wash, drain and chop fine:
> *1 bunch fresh basil (4 cups, loosely packed) or use half basil, half parsley*

Combine basil in a blender or processor with:
> *¼ cup olive oil*

Blend, add and blend in:
> *½ cup toasted pine nuts or   2 cloves garlic, minced*
> *walnuts, ground   1½ Tbsp. light miso*

Let sit for 30 minutes while you cook the pasta.

Cook until tender:
> *12 oz. pkg. linguine or fettucine*

Add a little of drained water from cooked pasta to dilute the pesto. Pour over the hot, drained pasta.

Per serving: Calories: 462, Protein: 10 gm., Carbohydrates: 54 gm., Fat: 12 gm.

SPINACH NOODLES

with Bechemel Sauce

In a large pot bring to a boil,
> *3 quarts water*

Add:
> *1 lb. spinach noodles*   *pinch of sea salt*

Cover and bring to a second boil. After second boil add, mixing in from top to bottom:
> *2 cups cold water*

Cover and bring to a boil. Cook 10-12 minutes. Taste noodles to see if done in center. Drain and rinse noodles with cold water several times until cooled (otherwise they will become soft).

For Bechemel Sauce, heat a pan, add and sauté:
> *1 Tbsp. sesame or sunflower oil*
> *¼ cup minced onion*

Stir in and cook until it lightly browns, stirring:
> *½ cup whole wheat pastry flour*

Add slowly, whisking out lumps:
> *2 ½ cups water*

Bring to a boil, cook 5 minutes, whisking occasionally. Add:
> *2 Tbsp. tamari*   *2 Tbsp. lemon juice*

Reduce heat and simmer 15 minutes. Cover and set aside.

In another pan, heat oil and add:
> *1 tsp. toasted sesame oil*   *2 carrots, sliced thinly*
> *1 cup onions, thinly sliced*

Sauté until onions are transparent. Add and sauté until bright green:
> *2 cups green cabbage leaves, shredded*
> *½ cup purple cabbage leaves, shredded*

Vegetables should be crisp-tender. Put cooked, drained noodles in an oiled casserole. Top with vegetables, cover with the sauce. Garnish with chopped parsley if desired. Cover with foil and bake at 350° for 25-30 minutes.

Per serving: Calories: 424, Protein: 16 gm., Carbohydrates: 78 gm., Fat: 7 gm.

Variation: Use corn or jerusalem artichoke noodles.

VITALIZING VEGETABLES

SEA VEGETABLES

● Indicates macrobiotic recipe

MOM'S STUFFED ARTICHOKES

Yield: 4 servings

Wash and drain:
> **4 medium artichokes**

Trim off stem and top leaves of artichokes, spread out leaves as much as possible.

Mix:

3 cloves chopped garlic	**½ cup bread crumbs**
½ cup grated soy parmesan cheese	**1 tsp. mixed herbs: oregano, marjoram, tarragon**

Sprinkle mixture on artichokes, tapping to settle crumbs.

Sprinkle with:
> **2 Tbsp. olive oil**   **1 Tbsp. lemon oil**

Place upright in a pan with ½ cup boiling water, cover and steam for 35 to 40 minutes, until fork-tender. Serve hot or cold, with Lemon Vinaigrette (pg. 76) or Tofu Tahini Dressing (pg. 75) as a dipping sauce.

Per serving: Calories: 182, Protein: 8 gm., Carbohydrates: 21 gm., Fat: 3 gm.

ORIENTAL MUSHROOMS

Yield: 6 servings

Sauté for 2 minutes:
> **2 Tbsp. safflower oil**   **¼ cup chopped onion**

Add and cook a few minutes:
> **1 lb. whole small mushrooms, rinsed**

Sprinkle over mixture until mushrooms are coated:
> **2 Tbsp. whole wheat flour**

Add:

1 cup vegetable stock	**1 Tbsp. mirin**
1 Tbsp. tamari	

Cook over medium heat about 4 minutes. Serve hot. If desired, sprinkle with toasted slivered almonds.

Per serving: Calories: 199, Protein: 8 gm., Carbohydrates: 32 gm., Fat: 5 gm.

CREAMED SHIITAKE MUSHROOMS

Yield: 4 servings

Sauté in a skillet a few minutes until mushrooms begin to brown and give off liquid:

1 Tbsp. oil

1½ cups fresh shiitake mushrooms, sliced or 5 large, dried shiitake mushrooms, soaked, sliced and drained

Remove mushrooms, add to skillet:

1 Tbsp. sunflower oil   **1 small onion, chopped fine**

Sauté onions until soft. Stir in:

½ cup whole wheat pastry flour

Cook and stir a few minutes until bubbly, add:

3 cups vegetable stock (or use leftover juice from garbanzos)

Whisk to keep out lumps. Stir over low heat until sauce thickens and bubbles.

Stir in mushrooms. Reduce heat to low, simmer a few minutes, add:

2 Tbsp. tamari

3 Tbsp. lemon juice or brown rice vinegar

Taste to adjust seasonings, adding a pinch of sea salt if needed. Serve over toast or cooked grains.

Per serving: Calories: 131, Protein: 3 gm., Carbohydrates: 14 gm., Fat: 7 gm.

GINGERED CHICKPEAS with KALE

Yield: 6 servings

Soak overnight in 4 cups water:

1 cup uncooked chickpeas

Drain, add 4 cups water and cook 1 to 1½ hours until tender. Drain. Heat skillet and sauté:

1 Tbsp. fresh ginger, chopped   **1 Tbsp. safflower oil**

                                      1 onion, chopped

Add chickpeas and:

¾ lb. kale, cooked   **2 Tbsp. Shoyu Vinaigrette**

2 Tbsp. tamari   **(pg. 130)**

Serve over cooked brown rice or noodles.

Per serving: Calories: 141, Protein: 9 gm., Carbohydrates: 20 gm., Fat: 3 gm.

ROASTED NEW POTATOES

Yield: 6 servings

Preheat oven to 425°. Scrub well:
24 small new red potatoes

Prick each several times with a fork. Put on a shallow baking pan:
¼ cup olive oil

Add potatoes and shake pan to coat them with oil. Bake 30 minutes or until tender. Sprinkle with sea salt or dulse and serve with chopped fresh parsley or green onions.

Per serving: Calories: 231, Protein: 4 gm., Carbohydrates: 34 gm., Fat: 2 gm.

HEALTHFUL POTATO CHIPS

Yield: 4 servings

A great alternative to fast food fries.

Preheat oven to 400°. Spread on a cookie sheet:
2 Tbsp. sunflower oil

Slice paper thin and arrange on sheet in a single layer:
4 baking potatoes or sweet potatoes

Bake 15 to 20 minutes until crisp and golden brown.

Per serving: Calories: 207, Protein: 4 gm., Carbohydrates: 33 gm., Fat: 7 gm.

SPAGHETTI SQUASH ☯

Yield: 4 to 6 servings

Place on a cookie sheet and bake at 375° for 35-40 minutes:
1 medium sized spaghetti squash

Cut open, insides should be soft. Remove seeds and fibers. Scrape out the pulp into a warm dish and toss with:
¼ cup soy parmesan cheese

Or sprinkle with cinnamon and nutmeg.

Per serving: Calories: 41, Protein: 4 gm., Carbohydrates: 6 gm., Fat: 1 gm.

BAKED STUFFED SWEET POTATOES

Yield: 6 servings

Scrub well, trim ends, pierce through center with a fork:
6 medium sweet potatoes

Bake at 400° 45-50 minutes until soft. Cut a long slice from one side of each. Scoop out pulp, leaving a shell. Mash pulp with:
3 Tbsp. honey
3 Tbsp. safflower oil
½ tsp. sea salt

Spoon into the shells. Set on an oiled baking dish and bake at 350° for 15-20 minutes to heat through before serving.

Per serving: Calories: 255, Protein: 3 gm., Carbohydrates: 46 gm., Fat: 7 gm.

SWEET POTATO TANGERINE CASSEROLE

Yield: 6 servings

Steam until tender, cut into 1″ slices:
6 medium sweet potatoes, scrubbed

Peel and separate into segments:
4 seedless tangerines

Combine in a sauce pan:
½ cup brown rice syrup or ¼   **½ cup water**
cup honey   **1 Tbsp. arrowroot**
½ cup apple juice   **1 Tbsp. safflower oil**

Cook over low heat until thickened, stirring. In an oiled casserole, arrange layers of potatoes and tangerines.

Top with:
½ tsp. cinnamon
½ cup broken pecans or walnuts

Pour sauce over, bake at 350° for 30 minutes.

Per serving: Calories: 326, Protein: 4 gm., Carbohydrates: 60 gm., Fat: 4 gm.

BUTTERNUT SQUASH PIE ☯

Yield: 6 servings

Prebake for 5 minutes at 350°:
> **1 single 9" Whole Wheat Pie Crust (pg. 132)**

For filling, cook until tender:
> **1 large butternut squash, cut into chunks**

Drain and puree in a food mill or mash thoroughly. Add:

3 Tbsp. water	**2 tsp. sesame oil**
1 Tbsp. mirin	**1 tsp. fresh ginger, grated**
1 Tbsp. tamari	**fine**

Spoon into pie shell and sprinkle with:
> **2 Tbsp. toasted sesame seeds or chopped pecans**

Bake 20-25 minutes at 350°.

Per serving: Calories: 267, Protein: 6 gm., Carbohydrates: 37 gm., Fat: 10 gm.

CRISPY BAKED SQUASH

Yield: 6 servings

Steam until tender but firm:
> **2 acorn or 1 butternut squash, cut into 1" cubes**

Mix in a bowl:
> **¼ cup tamari**
> **¼ cup oil**

Mix in another bowl:

1 cup wheat germ	**1 Tbsp. dulse**
⅓ cup nutritional yeast	**pinch of cayenne**
1 Tbsp. paprika	

Dunk squash first in tamari and oil mixture, then in the dry ingredients. Place in a flat oiled casserole dish. Cover and bake at 350° for 30 minutes. Uncover and bake 5 to 10 more minutes.

Per serving: Calories: 242, Protein: 8 gm., Carbohydrates: 28 gm., Fat: 11 gm.

STUFFED ACORN SQUASH ☯

Yield: 4 servings

Wash, cut in half and remove seeds from:
2 small acorn squash

Bake face down in a pan at 350° for 40-45 minutes. Heat skillet, add:
1 Tbsp. sesame oil

Sauté for 1 minute:
½ cup chopped onion
2 cloves garlic, minced

Add to pan and sauté a few minutes:
2 cups broccoli flowerets

Add and sauté 1 minute more:
½ cup chopped green onions
4 seitan balls*(1-1½ cups), cut in small chunks

Stuff squash halves. warm in oven if made ahead.

*Seitan (gluten) is available in health food stores, or substitute cubes of tofu.

Per serving: Calories: 446, Protein: 14 gm., Carbohydrates: 9 gm., Fat: 4 gm.

CABBAGE DELIGHT

Yield: 6 servings

Heat a large pan and sprinkle with:
1 Tbsp. toasted sesame oil

Over medium heat, sauté a few minutes:
1 Tbsp. fresh ginger, chopped
1 chopped onion

Add and cook for 10 minutes, stirring occasionally:
3 cups chopped green cabbage
2 cups chopped red cabbage

Stir in:
¼ cup Lemon Vinaigrette (pg. 76)

Per serving: Calories: 112, Protein: 1 gm., Carbohydrates: 6 gm., Fat: 4 gm.

STUFFED BAKED TOMATOES

Yield: 6 servings

Wash, scoop out hollow on stem end, remove pulp, leaving shell:
> **6 medium tomatoes**

Sauté over medium heat until soft:
> **½ cup onion, chopped** **½ cup green onions, chopped**
> **½ cup red pepper, chopped** **2 tsp. sesame oil**

Mix together:
> **tomato pulp, mashed** **1 Tbsp. tamari**
> **½ lb. tofu, mashed** **1 Tbsp. basil**
> **1 cup cooked brown rice** **pinch of cayenne**
> **¼ cup parsley, chopped**

Combine cooked vegetables with tofu mixture. Stuff tomatoes and place in lightly oiled baking pan. Bake at 375⁰ for 20-25 minutes.

Per serving: Calories: 118, Protein: 6 gm., Carbohydrates: 17 gm., Fat: 3 gm.

GREEN BEANS with CASHEWS

Yield: 6 servings

Heat a large pot of water to boiling, add:
> **1 lb. young green beans** **a pinch of kelp**

Cook about 5 minutes, until crisp-tender. Drain. Trim green beans, cutting in half diagonally.

Over medium high, heat in skillet:
> **1 Tbsp. sesame oil** **1 tsp. dark sesame oil**

Add:
> **1 tsp. fresh ginger, chopped**
> **½ cup roasted cashews, sliced**

Stir fry 1 minute. Add drained beans and:
> **1 Tbsp. tamari** **½ tsp. garlic powder**

Serve hot.

Per serving: Calories: 110, Protein: 3 gm., Carbohydrates: 7 gm., Fat: 4 gm.

SPROUTS with SESAME SAUCE

Yield: 6 servings

Rinse and drain:
> **1 lb. fresh mung bean sprouts**

Mung bean or lentil sprouts are best.

Cut into 1″ sticks and parboil for 30 seconds, then drain:
> **1 large carrot**

Chop:
> **2 green onions with tops**

Toast in a hot dry skillet until they begin to pop:
> **2 Tbsp. sesame seeds**

Grind seeds in a suribachi. Place in a bowl with:

2 Tbsp. honey or ¼ cup brown rice syrup	**2 Tbsp. brown rice or apple cider vinegar**
1 Tbsp. tamari	**1 Tbsp. sesame oil**

Mix sauce, then toss with sprouts, carrots and onions.

Per serving: Calories: 90, Protein: 3 gm., Carbohydrates: 12 gm., Fat: 3 gm.

DELICATA SQUASH ☯

Yield: 2 large servings

If you don't find this oblong green squash with yellow stripes, use zucchini.
Preheat oven to 375⁰. Cut in half, scoop out seeds from:
> **1 delicata squash**

Cover squash with foil, place in oven and bake for 15 minutes while making stuffing.

Heat oil in pan and sauté:

¼ cup onion, minced	
1 clove garlic, minced	**2 tsp. safflower oil**

Add:

2 Tbsp. walnuts, chopped	**¼ cup mushrooms, chopped**
Dash each of tamari, marjoram, dulse and ginger	

Fill halves with mixture, cover with foil and bake another 30 minutes. Serve with Miso-Walnut Sauce (pg. 104).

Per serving: Calories: 120, Protein: 8 gm., Carbohydrates: 8 gm., Fat: 9 gm.

COOKED GREEN SALAD

Yield: 4 servings

Choose from a variety of nutritious, delicious greens, such as kale, collards, Swiss chard, bok choy, watercress, savoy or Chinese cabbage.

Wash well to remove any sand or sediment:
> **1 lb. greens**

Fill a large pan with water and a pinch of sea salt. Bring to a boil, drop in a few leaves at a time. Cook for a few seconds until leaves turn dark or bright green. Drain and dry. Cut up the leaves and sprinkle with roasted sesame seeds, a dash of tamari and a few drops of toasted sesame oil.

Per serving: Calories: 59, Protein: 5 gm., Carbohydrates: 6 gm., Fat: 1 gm.

SWEET PARSNIPS and BURDOCK

Yield: 4 servings

Heat skillet over medium heat, add:
> **1 Tbsp. dark sesame oil**

Add and sauté for a minute:
> **2 carrots, cut in 1" chunks**

Add and sauté 5-10 minutes:
> **2 large parsnips, cut in half-moon slices**
> **1 stalk burdock, cleaned, sliced**

Add to pan:
> **1 Tbsp. tamari**   **¼ cup water**

Cover, turn heat to low and cook another 10 minutes. When carrots can be pierced with a fork, vegetables are done.

Per serving: Calories: 116, Protein: 2 gm., Carbohydrates: 19 gm., Fat: 4 gm.

SEA VEGETABLES

A macrobiotic diet calls for 2 tablespoons of sea vegetables daily.

HIJIKI VEGETABLE PIE

Yield: 6 servings

Prebake for 5 minutes at 350°:
a 9" Whole Wheat Pie Crust shell (pg. 132)

Soak in water to cover for 5 minutes:
¼ cup dried hijiki

Drain, cut hijiki into small pieces. Heat in a skillet:
1 Tbsp. sesame oil

Sauté the hijiki for 2 minutes with:
3 cloves garlic, minced
1 medium onion, chopped

Add and sauté for 5 minutes:
1 cup cauliflower pieces
½ cup carrots, diced

Add seasonings:
1 Tbsp. powdered dulse   **¼ tsp. basil**
¼ tsp. oregano   **dash of cayenne**
¼ tsp. cumin

Combine in processor or blender:
1 lb. tofu, crumbled   **¼ cup parsley, chopped**
½ cup water   **¼ cup light miso**
¼ cup tahini   **1 Tbsp. rice syrup**

Process until creamy smooth. Mix together and blend in:
½ cup water
3 Tbsp. arrowroot

If using a blender, make in two batches, then stir together. Place vegetable and hijiki mixture in bottom of pie shell. Pour creamy tofu mixture over vegetables. Bake at 350° for 35-40 minutes.

Per serving: Calories: 219, Protein: 11 gm., Carbohydrates: 18 gm., Fat: 19 gm.

SESAME KOMBU

Yield: about 1 cup

See photo between pgs. 80-1.

Soak in water to cover for 15 minutes:
> **20" piece of kombu or wakame**

Wipe kombu off with paper towel, and cut in small squares.

Bring to a boil:
> **½ cup water**

Drop in and cook for 1 minute:
> **6-8 scallions, sliced in ¼" rounds**

Drain, rinse with cold water and squeeze out excess liquid.

Mix together in a bowl:
> **2 Tbsp. light miso**
> **2 Tbsp. tahini**
> **⅓ cup water**

Add scallions and kombu to miso mixture. Serve as a side dish at room temperature or chilled.

Per 2 Tbsp. serving: Calories: 40, Protein: 1 gm., Carbohydrates: 3 gm., Fat: 5 gm.

ARAME and CARROTS

Yield: 4 servings

One ounce of dried arame will expand to 2 cups when cooked.

Wash and soak in water to cover 5 to 10 minutes:
> **½ pkg. arame (25 gms.)**

Lift arame out carefully to leave any sand on the bottom of the water. Squeeze out water, cut arame into 2" lengths.

Heat:
> **2 tsp. toasted sesame oil**

Sauté arame for 5 minutes. Add and cook 2 minutes:
>   **2 carrots, cut in matchsticks**
>   **1 onion, cut in long thin slices**

Cover, bring to a boil. Reduce heat and simmer for 30 minutes. Remove cover.

Add:
>   **1-2 Tbsp. tamari**

Cook uncovered until liquid is evaporated. The taste should be slightly salty.

Per serving: Calories: 100, Protein: 3 gm., Carbohydrates: 18 gm., Fat: 3 gm.

Variation: In the summer, add 1 cup fresh sweet white corn.

MIXED VEGETABLES
with Lemon Spirulina Sauce
Yield: 6 servings

Heat in large pan and add:
>   **1 cup chopped onion**
>   **2 Tbsp. sesame oil**
>   **3 cloves garlic, minced**

Sauté until soft, add:
>   **2 cups broccoli flowers**   **½ cup chopped zucchini**
>   **¾ cup water or stock**   **½ cup chopped carrot**

Cover and simmer 10 minutes, until crisp tender. Add:
>   **juice of 1 lemon (¼ cup)**
>   **2 Tbsp. tamari**
>   **1 tsp. grated lemon rind**

Mix together, then stir into vegetables:
>   **3 Tbsp. whole wheat flour**
>   **¼ cup cold water**

Stir and cook until sauce thickens. Stir in last:
>   **1 Tbsp. spirulina powder**

Mix well. Serve over brown rice or pasta.

Per serving: Calories: 90, Protein: 3 gm., Carbohydrates: 10 gm., Fat: 5 gm.

ARAME with SOBA NOODLES

Yield: 4 servings

Soak in a quart of water 5 to 10 minutes. Lift out, leaving sand on bottom and chop:
> *1 cup arame*

Cook according to directions on package:
> *1-8 oz. pkg. buckwheat soba noodles*

In a serving bowl, combine:

4 scallions, chopped	*1 Tbsp. toasted sesame oil*
2 Tbsp. mirin	*1 Tbsp. tamari*
1 Tbsp. fresh ginger, minced	*1 Tbsp. brown rice vinegar*

Toss with the drained noodles, add the chopped arame and:
> *3 Tbsp. toasted sesame seeds*

Serve warm or chilled.

Per serving: Calories: 257, Protein: 5 gm., Carbohydrates: 43 gm., Fat: 5 gm.

HIJIKI with SESAME SEEDS

Yield: about 1 cup

An ounce of hijiki expands to 4 times original size.

Soak in a quart of water for 5 minutes, drain and chop:
> *½ cup dried hijiki*

Roast in a dry skillet until toasted:
> *2 Tbsp. sesame seeds*

Remove seeds to a side dish. Add to a hot skillet:
> *1 Tbsp. dark sesame oil*

Sauté the chopped hijiki for 3-4 minutes with:
> *1 onion, chopped*

Stir in and simmer on low for 15 minutes:
> *2 Tbsp. mirin*
> *1 Tbsp. tamari*   *1 Tbsp. rice syrup*

Top with toasted sesame seeds. Serve hot or at room temperature.

Per 2 Tbsp. serving: Calories: 43, Protein: 1 gm., Carbohydrates: 4 gm., Fat: 2 gm.

APPEALING ACCOMPANIMENTS

● *Indicates macrobiotic recipe*

MOTHER NATURE'S APPLE BUTTER

Yield: 3 pints

A low calorie all fruit spread. Try it on breakfast pancakes or muffins.

See photo between pgs. 80-81.

Wash, core and cut up but do not peel:
> **4 lbs. apples**

Place in a large kettle with:
> **3 cups apple juice or cider**

Cover, bring to a boil on medium high heat, then reduce heat to low and simmer until apples are soft, 35-45 minutes, stirring occasionally. Put through a food mill or press through a sieve, discarding skins. Return fruit pulp to kettle, stir in:
> **2 tsp. cinnamon**   **½ tsp. ground cloves**
> **1 tsp. allspice**

Cook slowly 1 to 2 hours, stirring from time to time as it thickens. Pack in hot sterile jars or keep refrigerated.

Per 2 Tbsp.serving: Calories: 26, Protein: 0 gm., Carbohydrates: 6 gm., Fat: 0 gm.

CRANBERRY RAISIN SAUCE

Yield: about 2 ½ cups

Wash and drain:
> **2 cups cranberries**

Soak in 1 cup hot water for 5 minutes:
> **½ cup raisins**
> **¼ cup currants**

Add to cranberries, with:
> **½ cup water**   **pinch of sea salt**
> **¼ cup barley malt**   **2 Tbsp. agar agar flakes**

Bring to a boil, reduce heat to low and simmer 10 to 15 minutes or until berries begin to pop. Stir frequently to avoid burning. Pour into a mold. Place in refrigerator for at least 1 hour to jell firmly.

Per ¼ cup serving: Calories: 57, Protein: 1 gm., Carbohydrates: 15 gm., Fat: 0 gm.

GINGER PEAR CHUTNEY

See photo opposite pg. 128.   *Yield: 3 pints*

Have ready:
> **3 lbs. firm fresh pears (about 6 large)**
> **1 cup honey or 2 cups brown rice syrup**
> **1 green pepper, chopped small**
> **2 cloves garlic, chopped small**
> **2 jalapeño peppers, chopped small**
> **2 Tbsp. fresh ginger, chopped**
> **1 cup onions, chopped small**

> **1 cup apple juice**   **1 tsp. allspice**
> **1 cup apple cider vinegar**   **juice of 1 lemon**
> **½ cup raisins**   **rind of 1 lemon, finely shred-**
> **1 tsp. sea salt**   **ded**

Peel, core and chop the pears. Combine all ingredients in a large heavy-bottomed pan. Bring to a boil, then reduce heat to low and cook, uncovered, for about 2 hours. Stir frequently so it does not stick or scorch. It will thicken as it cooks. Pack while hot in small sterilized jars.

Per 2 Tbsp. serving: Calories: 65, Protein: 0 gm., Carbohydrates: 17 gm., Fat: 0 gm.

GOMASIO

Yield: about 1 cup

Wash and drain:
> **1 cup sesame seeds**

Roast in a heavy skillet over low to medium heat for 3-4 minutes, stirring constantly with a wooden spoon:
> **1 Tbsp. + 1 tsp. sea salt**

Pour into a suribachi and grind to a fine powder, or use a mortar and pestle.

Next, roast the sesame seeds over low heat, stirring and shaking the skillet from time to time so seeds brown evenly. When they give off a nutty fragrance, darken in color and begin popping, crush one between your thumb and forefinger. When the seed crushes easily, pour them into the suribachi and grind them with the salt, slowly and evenly, until each seed is half crushed. The mixture should not be too fine. Keep in a tightly sealed container in the refrigerator.

Per 1 tsp. serving: Calories: 18, Protein: 1 gm., Carbohydrates: 1 gm., Fat: 0 gm.

KETCHUP

Yield: about 2 cups

1 Tbsp. of commercial ketchup has 170 mg. of sodium as well as sugar and preservatives.

In a 3-quart saucepan, bring to a boil:

- **2 cups tomato juice**
- **2 stalks celery, with leaves**
- **1-6 oz. can low-salt tomato paste**
- **1-6 oz. can water**
- **2 cloves garlic, sliced**
- **1 bay leaf**
- **1 onion, cut up coarsely**
- **1 cup parsley**

Reduce heat and cook, covered, for 20 minutes. Remove bay leaf, press juice and vegetables through a sieve into a clean pan.

Add:

- **1 cup apple cider vinegar**
- **¼ cup honey or ½ cup brown rice syrup**
- **1 tsp. dry mustard**
- **1 tsp. allspice**
- **1 tsp. cinnamon**
- **½ tsp. kelp**
- **½ tsp. each mace and celery seed**
- **¼ tsp. cayenne**

Simmer, uncovered, over low heat for about 1½ hours, stirring occasionally as it thickens. Keep in a covered jar in refrigerator.

Per 2 Tbsp. serving: Calories: 22, Protein: 1 gm., Carbohydrates: 5 gm., Fat: 0 gm.

QUICK BARBECUE SAUCE

Yield: 2 cups

Saut in a 2 qt. pan until onions are tender:

- **2 Tbsp. sunflower oil**
- **1 sliced onion**

Add:

- **1 cup Ketchup (pg. 128)**
- **¼ cup molasses**
- **¼ cup wet mustard**
- **2 Tbsp. chili powder**
- **2 Tbsp. tamari**
- **1 tsp. garlic powder**

Stir, bring to a boil, reduce heat and simmer 10 minutes. Good sauce for burgers or Sloppy Ron's (pg. 51).

Per ¼ cup serving: Calories: 8, Protein: 1 gm., Carbohydrates: 12 gm., Fat: 4 gm.

Curried Lentils, pg. 91
Ginger Pear Chutney, pg. 127

BARBECUE SAUCE

Yield: 2 pints

Heat pan, add oil and sauté onion until tender.

¼ cup oil
1 large onion, diced

Add to pan:

2 cups tomato puree (16 oz. can)
1-6 oz. can low salt tomato paste
1-6 oz. can water
½ cup honey

¼ cup molasses
¼ cup cider vinegar
2 Tbsp. tamari
2 Tbsp. lemon juice
1 tsp. allspice
1 tsp. cayenne

Bring to a boil, then reduce heat to very low and cook uncovered an hour or more until thickness desired. Stir in:

2 Tbsp. tamari
2 Tbsp. lemon juice

Cook a few minutes more. Keep in refrigerator.

Per ¼ cup serving: Calories: 103, Protein: 1 gm., Carbohydrates: 18 gm., Fat: 4 gm.

SALSA VERDE

Yield: ¾ cup

Combine in a blender or processor:

1 cup parsley, chopped (or use ½ cup parsley and ½ cup watercress)
½ cup olive oil
1 Tbsp. onion, minced

2 Tbsp. lemon juice
1 tsp. dijon mustard
1 tsp. tamari
1 clove garlic, minced

Blend thoroughly, chill. Serve cold on steamed vegetables or pasta.

Per 2 Tbsp. serving: Calories: 163, Protein: 0 gm., Carbohydrates: 1 gm., Fat: 4 gm.

Grandma Brown's Carrot Cake, pg. 138
Festive Bundt Cake, pg. 139
Aduki Carob Brownies, pg. 142
Date Oat Squares, pg. 144

SHOYU VINAIGRETTE

Yield: ⅓ cup

Add zest to leftovers with this tangy sauce.

¼ cup shoyu or tamari
2 Tbsp. brown rice vinegar
2 Tbsp. mirin

1 clove garlic, minced
1 tsp. fresh ginger, grated
(opt.)

Per 1 tsp. serving: Calories: 4, Protein: 0 gm., Carbohydrates: 1 gm., Fat: 0 gm.

DAIRY-LESS SEED CHEESE

Yield: 1 cup

Combine in a glass container:

2 cups water
½ cup sunflower seeds

½ cup sesame seeds (hulled)

Cover loosely and set aside for 12 hours. Blend to a creamy sauce. Place jar in a dark cabinet for 12 hours. If any mold forms, scoop it off. Remove cheese, discard liquid in jar bottom. Refrigerate to stop fermentation, keep 3-4 days. Good in lasagne, stuffed shells or any dish where cottage cheese is called for.

Per 2 Tbsp. serving: Calories: 105, Protein: 4 gm., Carbohydrates: 4 gm., Fat: 1 gm.

DELECTABLE DESSERTS

● Indicates macrobiotic recipe

WHOLE WHEAT PIE CRUST

Yield: single or double crust

For a 2-crust pie, sift together:
> **2½ cups whole wheat pastry flour**
> **½ tsp. sea salt**

Mix together:
> **½ cup corn or walnut oil**
> **¼ cup cold soy milk**
> **2 Tbsp. mirin**

Stir in wet ingredients, adding a little water if needed to form a ball of dough. Divide in half. Chill in refrigerator 15-20 minutes. Place ball between two pieces of waxed paper. (Dampen counter so paper doesn't slide). Roll out to a 12″ circle. Remove top paper and fit crust into a 9″ pie plate. Roll top crust to cover filling.

For a single pie crust, mix together:
> **1¼ cups whole wheat pastry flour**
> **¼ tsp. sea salt**

Mix together:
> **¼ cup oil**
> **2-3 Tbsp. cold soymilk or water**
> **1 Tbsp. mirin**

Stir wet and dry ingredients together, shape into a ball. Chill 15 minutes. Roll out between two pieces of waxed paper. Remove top paper and fit crust into a 9″ pie pan. For prebaked crust, heat oven to 375°. Prick bottom and sides of crust to prevent bubbles. Bake 18-20 minutes until lightly browned. Cool.

Per serving: Calories: 126, Protein: 3 gm., Carbohydrates: 13 gm., Fat: 7 gm.

APPLE PIE

Yield: 6 servings

Have ready:
> **1 two-crust recipe for Whole Wheat Pie Crust (pg. 132)**

Cook with ½ cup water for 5 minutes:
> **2 lbs. apples, thinly sliced (5⅓ cups)**

Drain, set apples aside, return liquid to pan. Add:
> *3½ Tbsp. arrowroot*

Add apples to pan and stir in:
> *½ cup barley malt or rice
> syrup*
> *3 Tbsp. lemon juice*
> *2 tsp. coriander*
> *dash of nutmeg*
>
> *½ tsp. grated lemon rind*
> *¼ tsp. sea salt*
> *¼ tsp. cinnamon*

Cook until thickened. Pour into pastry filled pie pan, cover with a top crust. Seal edges by tucking under the bottom crust and crimping. Cut 4 slits near center of crust. Bake at 400° for 40-45 minutes. Place a baking sheet or aluminum foil under pie to catch any juice that boils over.

Per serving: Calories: 469, Protein: 7 gm., Carbohydrates: 71 gm., Fat: 19 gm.

Variation: Add ½ cup chopped walnuts or ½ cup raisins to apple mixture.

BANANA COCONUT CREAM PIE

Yield: 6 servings

Prepare and prebake for 10 minutes at 350°:
> *a single Whole Wheat Pie Crust, (pg. 132)*

Make filling by combining in a blender:
> *15 dates*
> *2 cups water*
> *⅔ cup raw cashews*
>
> *3 Tbsp. coconut, grated*
> *2 Tbsp. arrowroot*
> *1 tsp. vanilla*

Blend until creamy smooth. Place in sauce pan, bring to a boil. Boil for 1 minute over medium heat, stirring constantly. Cool. Pour half the filling into the prebaked shell. Slice over the filling:
> *2 bananas*

Then cover with remaining filling. Bake at 350° for 40 minutes. Sprinkle with:
> *3 Tbsp. flaked coconut*

Chill. For summer, partially freeze.

Per serving: Calories: 385, Protein: 7 gm., Carbohydrates: 49 gm., Fat: 13 gm.

PECAN PIE

Yield: 8 servings

Have ready:
> **a single crust Whole Wheat Pie Shell, baked (pg. 132)**

Roast in a 350° oven for 15-20 minutes:
> **2 cups pecans**

Combine in a sauce pan:
> **¾ cup rice syrup**   **4 tsp. egg replacer, dissolved**
> **¾ cup maple syrup**   **in ½ cup water**
> **2 Tbsp. safflower oil**

Bring to a gentle boil, sprinkle with:
> **2 Tbsp. agar agar flakes**

Stir constantly and simmer 5 minutes. Cool a little, pour into prebaked shell. Let sit for 15 minutes, sprinkle with the roasted pecans. Let cool another 45 minutes at room temperature. Chill in refrigerator.

Per serving: Calories: 427, Protein: 5 gm., Carbohydrates: 39 gm., Fat: 16 gm.

STRAWBERRY CREAM PIE

Yield: 8 servings

Have ready:
> **1 qt. of fresh strawberries or 20 oz. frozen berries, adding**
> **sweetener to taste**
> **a single unbaked Whole Wheat Pie Crust (pg. 132)**

Blend in a food processor or blender until smooth and creamy:
> **1 lb. tofu**   **2 Tbsp. arrowroot**
> **¾ cup brown rice syrup**   **1 tsp. vanilla**
> **⅓ cup oil**   **pinch of sea salt**
> **2 Tbsp. lemon juice**

Fold in berries, saving a few to place on top after baking. Pour into unbaked pie shell. Bake at 350° for 45 minutes or until firm to touch. Cool. Also good topped with slices of kiwi. Cut into 8 wedges.

Per serving: Calories: 279, Protein: 8 gm., Carbohydrates: 23 gm., Fat: 18 gm.

APRICOT PIE

Yield: 8 servings

For oat nut crust, whiz in blender until a coarse meal:
1½ cup rolled oats

Mix in a bowl with:
½ cup walnuts, chopped fine   **¼ cup apple juice**
                                    ¼ cup water

Let stand 30 minutes. Oil a 9″ pie pan and press mixture firmly into bottom and sides, using the back of a large spoon. Bake at 350° for 30 minutes, until edges begin to brown.

For filling, snip into small pieces with scissors dipped in cold water:
1 cup dried apricots

Place apricots in saucepan, add:
1½ cups apple juice

Bring to a boil, reduce heat and simmer 15 minutes until fruit is soft.

Sprinkle on top to dissolve:
2 Tbsp. kanten flakes

Stir in and cook over medium heat, stirring, 3 minutes. Set off heat to cool. When it begins to set, pour into baked pie shell. Chill. A circle of Whipping Topping (pg. 135) can be piped around the outer edges of the pie for a pretty service. This dessert can be made the day before.

Per serving: Calories: 227, Protein: 6 gm., Carbohydrates: 38 gm., Fat: 6 gm.

TOFU WHIPPED TOPPING

Yield: 1½ cups

Whiz in a blender or processor until creamy smooth:
½ lb. tofu   **2 Tbsp. lemon juice**
¼ cup safflower oil   **1 tsp. vanilla**
2 Tbsp. barley malt or honey   **pinch of salt**

Keep chilled.

Per ¼ cup serving: Calories: 123, Protein: 3 gm., Carbohydrates: 4 gm., Fat: 11 gm.

TOFU CHEESECAKE

Yield: 8 servings

For crust, mix:

½ cup whole wheat pastry flour	**3 Tbsp. crushed walnuts**
½ cup rye flour	**1 tsp. cinnamon**
½ cup brown rice flour	**pinch of sea salt**

Blend in with a fork:
> **2 Tbsp. safflower oil**

Add:
> **¼ cup fruit juice**

Crust will be crumbly. Reserve ¼ cup for topping and press remaining mixture into an oiled 9″ pie pan. Preheat oven to 350°.

For filling, simmer for 10 minutes in an uncovered pan:

1 vanilla bean, split lengthwise	**½ cup water**
1 cup apple juice	**½ cup chopped dried papaya or peaches**

Remove vanilla bean and combine fruit in blender or processor with:

1 lb. soft tofu	**2 Tbsp. arrowroot**
2 Tbsp. tahini	**1 tsp. shredded orange rind**

Make in two batches if necessary. Combine and pour into crust. Sprinkle with reserved crumbs. Bake at 350° for 40 minutes, until firm. Cool. Top with Fresh Fruit Glaze.

Per serving: Calories: 202, Protein: 7 gm., Carbohydrates: 27 gm., Fat: 8 gm.

FRESH FRUIT GLAZE

Yield: 4 cups

Bring to a boil in a heavy sauce pan:
> **1 cup apple juice**

Add:
> **3 cups crushed fresh pineapple, peaches or blueberries, drained**
> **pinch of sea salt**

Bring to a boil. Cover and simmer 15 minutes. dilute:

>**2 Tbsp. arrowroot**
>**2 Tbsp. water**

Add to cooked fruit and simmer 5 minutes or until thick, stirring. Taste for sweetness. Cool. Spread on top of cooled pie. Chill.

Per ½ cup serving: Calories: 44, Protein: 0 gm., Carbohydrates: 11 gm., Fat: 0 gm.

GINGER CAKE
with Lemon Sauce

Yield: 9 servings

Combine in a food processor or mixing bowl:

>**2 cups whole wheat pastry flour**
>**2 tsp. powdered ginger**
>**½ tsp. sea salt**

Add:

>**½ cup honey**
>**¼ cup molasses**

Dissolve and add last, beating as you add:

>**1 tsp. baking soda in**
>**1 cup boiling water**

Spread evenly into a well-oiled 8″ x 8″ pan. Bake in a preheated oven at 350° for 30-35 minutes until sides begin to draw away from edge of pan. Cool, cut into 9 squares. Serve topped with warm lemon sauce.

For Lemon Sauce, bring to a boil:

>**¾ cup water**
>**¼ cup honey**

Mix together:

>**1 Tbsp. arrowroot**
>**¼ cup cold water**

Add the boiling water to the arrowroot mixture slowly, then return to pan and cook until thickened, stirring constantly.

Stir into sauce:

>**2 Tbsp. lemon juice**
>**2 tsp. grated lemon rind**

Per serving: Calories: 198, Protein: 4 gm., Carbohydrates: 48 gm., Fat: ½ gm.

GRANDMA BROWN'S CARROT CAKE

Yield: 16 servings

See photo opposite pg. 129.

Prepare 2 or 3 8″ round cake pans by cutting circles of waxed paper to line the bottom of the tins. Oil pan, then oil paper.

Mix the dry ingredients:

3 cups whole wheat pastry flour
2½ tsp. baking soda

2 tsp. cinnamon
½ tsp. sea salt

Have ready:

3 cups grated carrots
1 cup rice syrup or ½ cup honey
⅔ cup safflower oil

2 tsp. vanilla
4 tsp. egg replacer dissolved in ¾ cup water

Stir together the sweetener, oil, egg replacer in water and vanilla. Add the dry ingredients. Fold in the grated carrots. Pour into cake pans. Preheat oven to 350° and bake for 25 to 30 minutes. Cool, remove layers. make a double recipe of Tofu Whipped Topping (pg. 135) but do not double the lemon juice. Spread between layers and top of cake. Decorate with hazelnuts or pecans if desired.

Per serving: Calories: 240, Protein: 3 gm., Carbohydrates: 37 gm., Fat: 10 gm.

CAROB CAKE

Yield: 1 9″ x 13″ pan (15 servings)

Oil a 9″ x 13″ pan and dust bottom of pan lightly with carob powder. Mix in a large bowl:

2 cups wholewheat pastry flour (or use half unbleached white flour)
½ cup carob powder
2 tsp. baking powder

½ tsp. baking soda

Make a well in center of dry ingredients and add:

1 cup soy milk
½ cup honey or 1 cup brown rice syrup

½ cup safflower oil
1 tsp. vanilla

Mix wet and dry ingredients together well, pour into prepared pan. Preheat oven to 350° and bake about 30 minutes or until top of cake springs back when gently pressed. Cool, sprinkle with coconut before serving.

Per serving: Calories: 167, Protein: 3 gm., Carbohydrates: 24 gm., Fat: 8 gm.

Variation: Arrange 20 pecan halves on top of dough before baking so each serving will be topped with a pecan.

FESTIVE BUNDT CAKE

Yield: 16 slices

See photo opposite pg. 129.

Prepare a bundt pan by oiling carefully and dusting with flour. Mix in a bowl and let stand 10 minutes:
> **1½ cups boiling water**
> **1 cup raisins**
> **½ cup currants**

Stir in:
> **2 cups apples, peeled, cored and grated**
> **2 cups rice syrup or 1 cup honey**
> **¼ cup safflower oil**

In another bowl mix:
> **2½ cups whole wheat flour**   **1 tsp. cinnamon**
> **¼ cup soy flour**   **1 tsp. allspice**
> **1½ tsp. baking soda**   **½ tsp. nutmeg**

Roast at 350° for 15 minutes:
> **1 cup chopped pecans**

Combine with apple mixture. Mix wet and dry ingredients. Pour into prepared bundt pan. Bake at 325° 45-50 minutes or until done. Cool 10 minutes. Remove from pan. Place on serving plate. Pulverize **1 cup coconut** in blender and sprinkle on top. Or brush top with glaze made of:
> **2 Tbsp. lemon juice**
> **2 Tbsp. rice syrup or honey**
> **2 Tbsp. water**

Decorate with blanched almond halves or bits of dried fruit.

Per serving: Calories: 284, Protein: 5 gm., Carbohydrates: 47 gm., Fat: 7 gm.

ALL NATURAL FRUIT CAKE

Yield: 2 loaf pans

Make a holiday treat for yourself and one to give away.

Snip into small pieces with scissors:
> **1 cup dried papaya**
> **1 cup dried apricots**
> **½ cup dried pineapple**

Combine with;
> **½ cup currants**

Cover with:
> **2 cups apple juice or cider**

Bring to a boil, cover, turn off heat and let stand 15 minutes. Drain, saving liquid. Let cool. Prepare 2 loaf pans by cutting strips of waxed paper to line bottom and sides with paper overhang. Oil bottom of pans and oil paper.

Have ready:
> **1 cup chopped pecans**

Mix in a large bowl:
> **3½ cups whole wheat pastry**   **1 tsp. cinnamon**
> **flour**   **½ tsp. baking soda**
> **3 tsp. baking powder**   **½ tsp. sea salt**
> **1 tsp. nutmeg**   **½ tsp. mace**

Make a well in the center of the dry ingredients, add:
> **1 cup liquid drained from**   **½ cup honey**
> **fruit (add water to make 1**   **2 Tbsp. molasses**
> **cup if necessary)**   **1 tsp. vanilla**
> **½ cup oil**

Stir together and divide mixture into prepared pans. Heat oven to 300° and place a large pan of boiling water on bottom shelf. Bake cakes on middle shelf. After 1 hour, remove water, lay a piece of foil loosely over cakes if they are getting brown. Bake 30 minutes more. Remove from oven and cool, remove from pans and strip off waxed paper.

Per slice: Calories: 148, Protein: 2 gm., Carbohydrates: 23 gm., Fat: 4 gm.

CAROB PECAN COOKIES

Yield: 24 cookies

See photo between pgs. 80-81.

Grind in a processor or blender:
   1¼ cup rolled oats

If using a processor, add other ingredients. Or mix by hand the ground oats and:

1 cup whole wheat pastry   *½ tsp. baking powder*
   flour   *¼ tsp. sea salt*
½ cup carob powder

When dry ingredients are mixed, stir in:
   ½ cup safflower oil   *1 tsp. vanilla*
   ½ cup honey

Shape into 24 small balls (wet hands) and place on a lightly oiled cookie sheet. Press a pecan half or whole blanched almond on top of each. Bake at 350° for 10-12 minutes.

Per cookie: Calories: 121, Protein: 2 gm., Carbohydrates: 17 gm., Fat: 6 gm.

CAROB CHIP BLONDIES

Yield: 16 squares

Blend in a food processor:
   ½ lb. soft tofu, drained   *¼ cup safflower oil*
   ½ cup brown rice syrup   *1 tsp. vanilla*

Mix dry ingredients together:
   1½ cups whole wheat pastry   *½ cup whole wheat flour*
      flour   *2 tsp. baking powder*
   ½ cup walnut meal (crum-   *½ tsp. baking soda*
      bled in blender)

Add dry ingredients to food processor and blend. remove and stir in:
   1 cup carob chips
   ½ cup chopped walnuts

Spread into an oiled 9" x 9" pan. Bake at 350° for 25 minutes. Cool, cut into 16 squares.

Per square: Calories: 229, Protein: 7 gm., Carbohydrates: 24 gm., Fat: 13 gm.

COUSCOUS CRUNCH BARS

Yield: 24 bars

Whiz in blender:
1¼ cups rolled oats

Mix in a bowl with:
1 cup whole wheat pastry flour
2 tsp. baking powder
pinch of sea salt

Mix together, then combine with dry ingredients:
1 cup apple juice
¼ cup water
¼ cup safflower oil
2 Tbsp. brown rice syrup

1 tsp. egg replacer in 1 Tbsp.
water
1 tsp. vanilla

Stir into batter:
2 cups cooked couscous or millet

Pour batter into oiled 9″ x 13″ baking pan. Preheat oven to 350°.

Combine in a small bowl for topping:
¼ cup apple juice
¼ cup almond or cashew
butter
¼ cup coconut

2 Tbsp. sesame seeds, toasted
1 tsp. cinnamon
½ tsp. nutmeg

Mix in:
½ cup chopped walnuts

Spread topping over batter. Bake at 350° for 40-45 minutes. Cut into squares.

Per serving: Calories: 125 Protein: 3 gm., Carbohydrates: 14 gm., Fat: 6 gm.

ADUKI CAROB BROWNIES

Yield: 24 brownies

See photo opposite pg. 129.

Rinse in cold water and discard any shrivelled beans:
1 cup dried aduki beans

Bring to a boil with:

> **2 cups water**
> **1 cup apple juice**
> **1 vanilla bean, split**

Cover, reduce heat and cook until beans are tender, adding more liquid if necessary (45 minutes under pressure, 2 hours in a covered kettle). Remove vanilla, mash beans until creamy.

Blend into beans:

> **1 cup chopped walnuts**　　　**½ cup buckwheat flour**
> **1 cup whole wheat pastry**　　**½ cup safflower oil**
> **　flour**　　　　　　　　　　**1 tsp. cinnamon**
> **1 cup applesauce**　　　　　 **½ tsp. baking soda**
> **½ cup carob powder**　　　　**¼ tsp. sea salt**

Preheat oven to 350°. Spoon into a well-oiled 9″ x 15″ cake pan. bake 25-30 minutes or until firm.

Per serving: Calories: 100, Protein: 4 gm., Carbohydrates: 15 gm., Fat: 3 gm.

Variation: Reduce walnuts to ½ cup and add ½ cup raisins.

CAROB SUNFLOWER BALLS ☯

Yield: 20 balls

See photo between pgs. 80-81.

Spread in a single layer and toast at 350° for 10-15 minutes:

> **½ cup sunflower seeds**
> **½ cup walnuts**

Chop walnuts finely, mix with seeds and:

> **1 cup almond or cashew**　　**½ cup rolled oats**
> **　butter**　　　　　　　　　　**¼ tsp. vanilla**
> **½ cup brown rice syrup**　　 **1 Tbsp. sesame seeds**
> **½ cup carob powder**

Wet hands and shape mix into 2 inch balls. Roll in:

> **¾ cup shredded coconut**

Crushed almonds can be used instead of coconut. Chill.

Per serving: Calories: 166, Protein: 4 gm., Carbohydrates: 13 gm., Fat: 6 gm.

OATMEAL CAROB CHIP COOKIES

Yield: 4 dozen

Mix together:
> **3 cups rolled oats**
> **1¼ cups whole wheat pastry**
> **flour**

> **¼ cup flaked coconut**
> **½ tsp. baking soda**

Mix in another bowl:
> **2 cups cold water**
> **½ cup rice syrup**
> **3 Tbsp. safflower oil**

Have ready:
> **¾ cup unsweetened carob chips**
> **½ cup chopped walnuts or pecans**

Pour wet ingredients over oat-flour mixture, mix well and stir in chips and nuts. Preheat oven to 375°. Spoon batter onto oiled cookie sheets, press flat. Bake 20-25 minutes.

Per cookie: Calories: 82, Protein: 2 gm., Carbohydrates: 12 gm., Fat: 13 gm.

Variation: Use 1 cup water and 1 cup apple juice for liquid and reduce rice syrup to ⅓ cup.

DATE OAT SQUARES

Yield: 16 squares

See photo opposite pg. 129.

Place in blender and pulverize:
> **2 cups rolled oats**

Mix with:
> **1 cup whole wheat pastry flour**
> **¼ tsp. sea salt**
> **grated rind of 1 lemon**

Stir in and mix until crumbly:
> **⅓ cup barley malt or ¼ cup honey**
> **¼ cup oil**

Pat ⅔ of the dough into an oiled 9″ x 9″ pan. Spoon the fruit topping on evenly, sprinkle remaining dough on top. Preheat oven to 350° and bake for 35-45 minutes.

For topping, combine in a saucepan:

> **1½ cups chopped dates**
> **⅔ cup water**
> **pinch of sea salt**

> **½ cup barley malt or ¼ cup honey**
> **juice of 1 lemon**

Simmer the fruit in water until soft. Mash with lemon juice, salt and sweetener. Spread on crust and bake as above.

Per serving: Calories: 189, Protein: 4 gm., Carbohydrates: 34 gm., Fat: 5 gm.

Variation: Use figs, taste filling and add sweetener if needed.

BREAD PUDDING

Yield: 6 servings

Cut bread into 1″ cubes. Place in a bowl:

> **3 cups whole wheat bread cubes, firmly packed**
> **½ cup currants**

Pour over the bread and soak 15 minutes:

> **1 cup water**
> **1½ cups apple juice**

Press bread to drain off excess liquid, add liquid to processor or blender with:

> **½ lb. tofu**
> **2 Tbsp. roasted sunflower seeds**

> **1 tsp. vanilla**
> **¼ tsp. nutmeg**
> **pinch of sea salt**

Blend until creamy. Combine tofu and soaked bread and place in an oiled casserole dish. Sprinkle with cinnamon. Bake uncovered at 350° for 45 minutes. Serve warm or chilled. Top with toasted sunflower seeds, if desired. Good with Tofu Whipped Topping (pg. 135)

Per serving: Calories: 307, Protein: 11 gm., Carbohydrates: 55 gm., Fat: 4 gm.

ROYAL RICE PUDDING

Yield: 6 servings

Mix together:

3 cups cooked brown rice or quinoa
½ cup currants or raisins
½ cup dried papaya (opt.)
½ cup slivered toasted almonds
Pinch each of nutmeg and cloves or allspice

1 cup apple juice	**½ tsp. vanilla**
1 cup water	**½ tsp. cinnamon**
2 Tbsp. tahini	**½ tsp. grated lemon rind**

If quinoa is used, reduce liquid by ½ to 1 cup. For a sweeter pudding, mix in ¼ cup barley malt or honey. Turn mixture into an oiled casserole.

Top with:
½ cup toasted sesame seeds

Bake uncovered at 350° for 30 minutes.

Per serving: Calories: 325, Protein: 8 gm., Carbohydrates: 39 gm., Fat: 10 gm.

Date Pudding: Instead of raisins or currants, use 1 cup pitted cut up dates, use ½ cup chopped walnuts instead of almonds.

CAROB PUDDING

Yield: 6 servings

Mix in a food processor or blender until creamy and smooth:

1 lb. tofu	**½ cup carob powder**
½ cup safflower oil	**1 Tbsp. lemon juice**
½ cup rice syrup or ¼ cup honey	**2 tsp. vanilla**

Spoon into dessert dishes, cover and chill. For a festive presentation, put pudding into tall glass dishes, chill. Top each with Tofu Whipped Topping (pg. 135) and dot with carob chips. Or top with slivered toasted almonds.

Per serving: Calories: 283, Protein: 7 gm., Carbohydrates: 22 gm., Fat: 22 gm.

DEBBIE'S OATMEAL FRUIT PIE

Yield: 6 servings

Any combination of fruit is good and a great way to use leftover cold oatmeal.

Make oatmeal by combining:

2½ cups rolled oats   **pinch of sea salt**
2 cups water

Bring to a boil, stirring constantly for 1 minute to keep it from burning. Turn off heat, stir. Cool. Lightly oil a 9″ pie pan.

Mix with the oatmeal:

2 cups (16 oz.) blueberries or other fresh or frozen fruit
    (unsweetened)
¼ cup wheat germ   **¼ cup honey or rice syrup**
½ banana, sliced   **½ tsp. cinnamon**
¼ cup chopped walnuts or
    cashews

Spread mixture in pan and bake at 350° for 30 to 40 minutes. Serve warm or cold.

Per serving: Calories: 357, Protein: 11 gm., Carbohydrates: 64 gm., Fat: 7 gm.

BAKED PEARS with Pecans

Yield: 4 servings

Peel, cut each in half and remove core from:
4 firm pears

Place core side up on a lightly oiled baking dish. Mix:
½ cup chopped pecans
½ cup barley malt or ¼ cup honey

Put a large spoonful in center of each pear. Sprinkle with:
1 tsp. ground ginger   **¼ tsp. nutmeg**

Pour into pan:
½ cup apple or pear juice

Bake pears at 350° for 20 to 30 minutes, until tender. Serve 2 halves on a plate, spooning pan juices over them.

Per serving: Calories: 270, Protein: 2 gm., Carbohydrates: 48 gm., Fat: 3 gm.

BAKED STUFFED APPLES

Yield: 4 servings

Have ready:
> **4 apples, core removed**

Heat oven to 350°. Cover bottom of pie pan with:
> **¼ cup apple juice**

Mash together:
> **½ lb. tofu**
> **½ tsp. cinnamon**
> **¼ tsp. each nutmeg and allspice**

Have ready:
> **½ cup granola**   **12 raisins**

Place apples in pie pan, put a little granola in each, then tofu mixture, 3 raisins, tofu mixture, top with granola. Sprinkle over top:
> **¼ cup apple juice**

Bake uncovered 35-40 minutes or until apples are soft.

Per serving: Calories: 219, Protein: 7 gm., Carbohydrates: 36 gm., Fat: 6 gm.

FRUIT KABOBS

Yield: 12 kabobs

See photo between pgs. 80-1. Marinating fruit will retain a fresh color if made ahead.

Have ready:
> **3 red pears or apples**   **½ fresh pineapple**
> **1 honey dew melon**

Mix for a marinade:
> **½ cup orange juice**   **1 Tbsp. lemon juice**
> **¼ cup water**

Core pears or apples but do not peel. Cut into 1″ chunks and marinate so they do not turn brown. Cut pineapple in cubes. Use a melon baller, or cut melon into chunks. Soak until serving time in juices. Thread onto 7″ wooden skewers. Arrange on platter or stick skewers into half a grapefruit.

Per kabob: Calories: 41, Protein: 1 gm., Carbohydrates: 10 gm., Fat: 0 gm.

APPLE CRISP

Yield: 6 servings

Place in an oiled, shallow baking pan:
> **4 cups sliced apples**

Sprinkle with:
> **1 tsp. grated lemon rind**

Combine and mix until crumbly:

1¼ cups rolled oats	**2 Tbsp. sesame seeds**
⅓ cup whole wheat pastry flour	**1 tsp. cinnamon**
¼ cup walnuts, chopped	**½ tsp. nutmeg**

Stir together:

2 Tbsp. water	**2 Tbsp. lemon juice**
2 Tbsp. oil	

Mix wet and dry ingredients. Sprinkle over apples. Bake at 350° for 30 minutes, until apples are tender.

Per serving: Calories: 281, Protein: 7 gm., Carbohydrates: 40 gm., Fat: 10 gm.

Orange Apple Crisp: Use ¼ cup orange juice instead of water and lemon juice and 2 tsp. grated orange rind instead of lemon rind.

Peach Crisp: Use 4 cups sliced peaches, in season. Omit lemon rind and cinnamon. If peaches are not sweet, sprinkle them with ¼ to ½ cup of barley malt.

STUFFED PINEAPPLE SHELL

Yield: 7 cups

Cut in half lengthwise and cut out the flesh, leaving a ½" thick shell.
> **1 firm, ripe pineapple, with leaves left on**

Cut core off flesh, cut up fruit and mix with:

1 cup watermelon or honeydew balls	**1 cup blueberries or strawberries**
1 cup cut up peaches	

Pile mixed fruit back into the shells, cover with plastic and refrigerate until serving time. Garnish each with mint sprigs.

Per ½ cup serving: Calories: 42, Protein: 1 gm., Carbohydrates: 10 gm., Fat: 0 gm.

FRUIT KANTEN

Yield: 6 servings

Have ready:
> **2 pears or apples, thinly sliced**

Bring to a boil:
> **1 cup apple or pear juice**
> **1 cup water**

Stir in and simmer 5 minutes:
> **2 Tbsp. agar-agar flakes**

Add:
> **1/8 tsp. sea salt**

Add fruit. Return to a boil and cook 3 minutes. Pour into a mold or dessert dish and let gel at room temperature or refrigerate for 45 minutes. To unmold, invert mold on plate and leave at room temperature 1 hour before serving.

Per serving: Calories: 54, Protein: 0 gm., Carbohydrates: 14 gm., Fat: 0 gm.

Variations: Try with different fruits. Banana and orange slices are good, or strawberries and kiwi. A nice addition is ⅓ cup raisins; plump them in ½ cup boiling water and drain before adding. For a sweeter dessert, cook ¼ cup barley malt or 2 Tbsp. honey with the juice.

ROY'S PEACH COBBLER

Yield: 6 servings

Preheat oven to 400°. Oil an 8″ x 8″ pan. Layer on bottom:
> **3 cups cut up peaches**

Mix for a dough:
> **2 cups whole wheat pastry flour**
> **1 cup soymilk**
> **¼ cup oil**
> **¼ cup barley malt or 2 Tbsp. honey**
> **4 tsp. baking powder**

Spread batter over fruit. Bake 25-30 minutes. Serve hot. Good with a dollop of non-dairy ice cream.

Per serving: Calories: 347, Protein: 7 gm., Carbohydrates: 61 gm., Fat: 10 gm.

APPLE RINGS ☯

Yield: 2 servings

Core:
> **1 apple**

Stuff with:
> **2 Tbsp. almond or sunflower butter**

Chill and slice.

Per serving: Calories: 124, Protein: 7 gm., Carbohydrates: 19 gm., Fat: 4 gm.

BANANA TREATS

Yield: 2 servings

Slice into chunks:
> **1 banana**

Dip into:
> **2 Tbsp. fruit juice**

Then roll in:
> **2 Tbsp. crushed walnuts or granola**

Delicious frozen.

Per serving: Calories: 24, Protein: 5 gm., Carbohydrates: 32 gm., Fat: 8 gm.

CAROB DUNKING SAUCE

Yield: 8 servings

Have fruit ready to dunk:
> **1 qt. fresh or frozen strawberries, or chunks of 4 bananas on skewers.**

Combine in a saucepan and cook over very low heat, stirring:

> **10 oz. unsweetened carob chips**
> **¾ cup soymilk**
> **½ cup brown rice syrup**
>
> **1 tsp. vanilla**
> **½ tsp. cinnamon**
> **¼ tsp. nutmeg**

Cook until chips are melted and mixture is smooth, about 15 minutes. Place fruit on fondue forks to dip into sauce. Other fresh or frozen fruits can be used.

Per serving: Calories: 271, Protein: 8 gm., Carbohydrates: 36 gm., Fat: 15 gm.

BANANA BON BONS

Yield: 4 servings

Melt:
> **½ cup unsweetened carob chips**
> **2 Tbsp. of brown rice syrup.**

Dip into melted carob mix:
> **1 banana, cut into chunks**

Roll coated chunks in:
> **¼ cup chopped nuts**

Freeze.

Per serving: Calories: 195, Protein: 5 gm., Carbohydrates: 23 gm., Fat: 11 gm.

LO-CAL CHEEZIE POPCORN

Yield: 3 cups

Pop with any popcorn maker that doesn't require oil:
> **⅓ cup of popcorn**

Sprinkle it with:
> **yellow cheesy-tasting nutritional yeast.**

You can eat three cups of this tasty popped corn for less than 100 calories!

One serving: Calories: 69, Protein: 2 gm., Carbohydrates: 14 gm., Fat: 1 gm.

MAPLED PECANS

Yield: about 2 cups

Combine in a skillet:
> **½ cup maple syrup**   **1 tsp. cinnamon**

Cook and stir over medium heat until mixture starts to thicken.

Stir in:
> **1 ½ tsp. vanilla**   **2 cups pecans**

Toss until evenly coated with glaze. Turn onto waxed paper to cool, separating with a fork. Store in airtight container in the refrigerator.

Per ¼ cup serving: Calories: 236, Protein: 3 gm., Carbohydrates: 17 gm., Fat: 5 gm.

FABULOUS CAROB FUDGE ☯

Yield: 16 squares

Combine in a sauce pan and heat over low, stirring until mixture blends easily:
1 cup nut butter (peanut, almond, cashew or sunflower)
1 cup rice syrup or barley malt

Stir in:
1 cup carob powder   **½ cup walnuts, chopped**

Pour into an oiled 8″ x 8″ pan and flatten into the corners. Cool in refrigerator. Cut into 16 squares.

Per square: Calories: 157, Protein: 5 gm., Carbohydrates: 19 gm., Fat: 5 gm.

TAMARI ALMONDS ☯

Yield: 1 cup

See photo between pgs. 80-81.

In a small bowl, mix and let stand an hour or so, stirring from time to time:
1 cup unblanched whole almonds   3 Tbsp. tamari

Spread on a baking sheet and bake at 350° for 10 minutes, until roasted. Store in a tightly covered jar.

Per ¼ cup serving: Calories: 227, Protein: 7 gm., Carbohydrates: 8 gm., Fat: 6 gm.

TOFU STRAWBERRY SMOOTHIE

Yield: 2 large glasses

Combine in a blender or processor:
¾ lb. soft tofu, crumbled   **1 ½ cups apple juice**

Blend, add:
1 frozen banana, sliced
10 frozen unsweetened strawberries

Put juice in blender, crumble in the tofu and blend. Drop in the frozen fruit and blend until creamy.

Per glass: Calories: 291, Protein: 15 gm., Carbohydrates: 45 gm., Fat: 8 gm.

INDEX

Tostadas, 52
triticale, 11

U

Udon Noodle Salad, 67
udon, 27
Umeboshi Dressing, 66
umeboshi plums, 27

V

Vegetable Chop Suey, 84
Vegetable Pie, Hijiki, 121
Vegetable Pizza, 99
Vegetable Soup, Hearty, 54
Vegetable Soup, Lentil, 58
Vegetable Stew, Black
  Bean and, 94
Vegetables, 17-20
Vegetarian Chili with
  Bulghur, 105
Vegetarian Lasagne, 107
Vegie Pie, Smith Valley
  Farms, 92
Vinaigrette, Lemon, 76
Vinaigrette, Shoyu, 130
Vitamin B12, 7

W

Waffles, Mochi, 40
Wakame Soup, Miso, 60
wakame, 20
Walnut Sauce, 104
wasabi, 27
wheat berries, 27
Wheat Berry Salad, Renee's 72
Whipped Topping, Tofu, 135
whole wheat, 10
  Biscuits, 45
  Croutons, 44
  English Muffins, 45
  pastry flour, 27
  Pie Crust, 132
Wild Grain Pilaf, 98

Z

Zucchini Salad, 74

Weights & Measures

3 tsp. = 1 Tbsp.
4 Tbsp. = ¼ cup
5⅓ Tbsp. = ⅓ cup
8 Tbsp. = ½ cup
1 lb. flour = 4 cups

8 fluid oz. = 1 cup
2 cups = 1 pint
16 fluid oz. = 1 pint
2 pints = 1 quart
4 quarts = 1 gallon

Metric Equivalents

1 Tbsp. = 14.8 ml.
1 cup = 236 ml.
1 quart = 946 ml.

1 oz. = 28 gm.
1 lb. = .454 kg.

Order these fine books directly from Book Publishing Company:

Tofu Cookery	$11.95
Tofu Quick and Easy	5.95
The Farm Vegetarian Cookbook	7.95
Judy Brown's Guide to Natural Foods Cooking	9.95
Kids Can Cook	8.95
Starting Over: Learning to Cook with Natural Foods	9.95
Vegetarian Cooking for Diabetics	9.95
Murrieta Hot Springs Vegetarian Cookbook	9.95
George Bernard Shaw Vegetarian Cookbook	8.95
Ten Talents	16.95
Spiritual Midwifery	16.95
A Coop Method of Natural Birth Control	5.95
The Fertility Question	5.95
No Immediate Danger	11.95
Shepherd's Purse: Organic Pest Control Handbook	5.95
Song of Seven Herbs	9.95
Dreamfeather	9.95
this season's people	5.95
A Basic Call to Consciousness	7.95
How Can One Sell the Air?	4.95

Please send $1 per book for postage and handling.

Mail your order to:
  Book Publishing Company
  PO Box 99
  Summertown, TN 38483